Spiritual Health And Healing

The Art of Living

Vedantin Ping Luo and Dennis Hill

School Yoga Institute
www.schoolyogainstitute.com
Turlock, CA 95382, USA

Order this book online at www.trafford.com
or email orders@trafford.com

Most Trafford titles are also available at major online book retailers.

© Copyright 2010 Vedantin Ping Luo and Dennis Hill.
Vedantin Ping Luo, Ed.D., E-RYT, Mystic Guide
All rights reserved. No part of this publication may be reproduced, stored in a retrieval system, or transmitted, in any form or by any means, electronic, mechanical, photocopying, recording, or otherwise, without the written prior permission of the author.

Printed in the United States of America.

ISBN: 978-1-4269-4622-6 (sc)
ISBN: 978-1-4269-4623-3 (e)

Our mission is to efficiently provide the world's finest, most comprehensive book publishing service, enabling every author to experience success. To find out how to publish your book, your way, and have it available worldwide, visit us online at www.trafford.com

Trafford rev. 10/08/2010

Trafford PUBLISHING   www.trafford.com

North America & international
toll-free: 1 888 232 4744 (USA & Canada)
phone: 250 383 6864 ♦ fax: 812 355 4082

Contents

Forward ix
Introduction to Spiritual Health and Healing xv
Difference between Religion and Spirituality xvi
Definition of Spiritual Being xvii
The Experiential Spiritual Health and Healing Lessons ... xix
"Letting Go" 1
Present Moment, Precious Moment 4
Surrender to 'What is' 8
Power of Thoughts 11
Mindfulness 17
Cosmic and Pure Love 21
Who Am I? 24
Meaning of Life 27
Active Listening – an Act of Generosity 31
Flow into Life 35
Action in Inaction and Inaction in Action 38
Experiential Embodiment 41
Form and Formlessness 45
Stillness Amidst the World 48

The All-Pervading Spirit of Satyagraha..........51
Listen to the Inner Voice 54
Be Indifferent 58
Transcendental Sexuality: Above and Beyond 62
Seasonal Celebrations 66
Don't Play Ego Roles..........70
Obtaining Mystical Consciousness 74
Homecoming 77
Playing the Edge 81
Spiritual Self Healing 85
Connecting to the All-Providing Source 90
Breaking Free from Samskara, the "Pain Body" 94
Lose Yourself Before You Find Your Self 97
Reveal the Love Within 100
Law of Attraction 103
Universal Space Within and Without..........106
The Law of Action and Reaction 109
Pursuing Happiness 114
Illusory Self 118
Portal of Enlightenment 121
Mystical Reunion 124
Compassionate Living 127
Shambhala 131
The Natural Bardo of Life 134
Sound Healing 138
Current of Divine Grace 141
You Are Bigger Than Your Egoic Self 144
Reaction to the World 148

Emotion: Bodily Expression of Thoughts in the Mind 152
Random Kindness 156
Connecting the Elements of the Universe............................159
Unavoidable Dramas – Manifestation of Divine Presence.........162
Getting Into the Zone 166
Luminous Being..170
Shedding Shadows..173
"Buy a Ticket" 176
Ritual 179
The Middle Path 182
Dreaming into Being 186
Art of Living 189
Senses of Non-Duality 192
Love 'n' Light 196
Walking in Beauty 199
Feed the Wolf 202
Dismemberment 204
Harmony 207
References and Recommended Readings 211

Forward

Upon my return from a three-month long spiritual journey at Lago Atitlan, the sacred Mayan lake in Guatemala, I entered into the world of the mundane, compounded with an unresolved relationship. My mind was filled with confusion, my inner state experienced discontentment, the purpose of my life was clouded, and my heart longed for clarity and wisdom. During a morning meditation a voice told me to go to Yosemite to search for the answer.

After I arrived at Yosemite National Park I asked the universe and my sacred beings, "Show me, let me experience, give me a vision, sign, or omen for how to live harmoniously with my intimate love-life without burden and heartache and live harmoniously within myself with contentment."

I got an answer, "Go fasting for the next three days, silencing for the next three days, sitting next to the water of a sacred place, and hear and commune with all spirits."

After two days of inner quest, long meditations, long yoga asana practices, long contemplations, and ceremonies, I thought I had obtained the "insights," but I still sensed incompletion.

"Insights"

- ✓ Listen to the voice of soul
- ✓ Distinguish the voice of soul from the voice of mind (surrender to the soul, discard the mind)
- ✓ Pay attention to the hidden treasure (handful of sand, giant grey squirrel hidden behind a tree, water tributaries merging into a creek, bird dancing on a rock, hidden sandy beach in front of the sacred inner-quest site, beyond the obvious)
- ✓ Follow my own soul journey undistracted by the world's conditions
- ✓ Take an inner quest during times of confusion and discontentment
- ✓ Be grateful to receive all of life's lessons, beauties and beasts, just like rocks, rivers, trees, sun …
- ✓ Communion with all beings with the language of soul
- ✓ Pay attention to a sign or omen and dare to take action beyond the doubt of mind
- ✓ Contemplate and meditate enough time with any beings, and the insights and visions will reveal

For sure, that happened to me when I was urged to leave the inner quest spot. But my mind said to me, "Stay, you have chosen this spot to gain the vision." But my heart wanted to have a stroll. I listened to my heart and strolled to a place where many tributaries merged into a rushing creek. I was wondering why I was there. My mind tried to convince me that I had had the insights, that the inner quest had been completed. But my heart said to me, "No, that is not it. You will know clearly when you have encountered such." I surrendered and stared at the rushing water, calming water, water between rocks, water currents, climbing water …

I Am Just Water

Flow through a creek
Rush down through a fall
Slip between rocks
Splash on shores
I am just water

Carve the mountains
Shape the rocks
Create sacred alters
I am just water

Run fast
Stroll slow
Create turbulences
Change color into white, black, green, and blue
I am just water

Fight upstream
Struggle through obstacles
Hide beneath
Suffer from poisoned mind
But I am still, just water

Surrender to gravity
Yield to the flow of the course
Take middle path
Turn left and right
I am just water

Shapeshift my identity
Into ice, ocean, glacier, rain, and fog
To serve
To live
I am just water

> Move the earth
> Feed all living or dying
> Coexist with all sentient beings
> On the earth
> I am just water
> Speak with soul
> The language we all know

Now I sensed the completion of my inner quest, with clarity and insight. I celebrated the inner quest with a break of fast. Surely I tasted the sweetness of life. I thought I had finished my inner quest yesterday but it is really just beginning.

I woke up super early in the forest. Seeing the moon go down and morning dawn set in. I sensed energy rising from within and started contemplating how to use my gifts to manifest in the world. So many new ideas were revealed and some renewed ones reappeared. I felt like a little baby who cannot wait to get into the world to share and experience. I am ready to take on the world duties once again with a sense of clarity and direction.

I walked down to the river for my morning sadhana practice and closely encountered with a nod a wild deer eating away its berries. A blue jay flew close by and just wanted to say hi. Everything was so quiet and serene that I was wondering if I was in the same place.

The meditation practice was divine, literally divine. I had no sense of time. The entire universe simply stopped for me to experience it. I felt I was in another realm of life.

Life in Another Realm

Vastness of space
Filled with clouds
And everything yet nothing
Quiet and calm
Changing shade
From bright to dark then to bright

In the dark
See stone walls
And many layers of doors
Come, come through here to see

Bright void
Melting snowy mountains
Dissolving dark mountains
Yet two sharp-edged, sandy glacial mountains
Hidden within the bright void

Sense of suspension
Sense of being
Sense of eternal
Sense of wonder
Sense of creation
Sense of indifference
Sense of belonging
Sense of nothingness

Sense
I am there
I am that

Roaring sound of mundane world
Chirping of birds
Gentle wind
Warm sun
Display in still
Everything stopped
So do the mind and the world

No desire to return
To the mundane
I know
I lived in another realm
(Goose bumps)
Is this the very end or very beginning of my inner quest?

Spiritual Health and Healing is a continuous process of inner quest for the truth, insights, clarity, and wisdom. When we open our hearts and step into our own soul journeys we will experience all the beauties and wonders in the world. May the wisdom of stories, teachings, and practices in this book give you guidance in leading you to the door of the unknown and the truth that can be verified by you and only by you.

Vedantin Ping Luo
California State University, Stanislaus
SchoolYoga Institute, USA
Mystical Yoga Farm, Guatemala

Introduction to Spiritual Health and Healing

'Spiritual health and healing' means using spiritual concepts of different traditions to reveal the true purpose of life. As human beings, we live in the world with a sense of duty and responsibility to society, and at the same time we experience the ultimate spiritual beings within our physical bodies. When we are in harmony with the mother earth, father sky, and the entire cosmos, we experience the right relationship with all that exists in the universe and we then reside in peace, joy, love and compassion. There is no more suffering or struggle. Even when suffering or struggles do exist, they solely serve to remind us that we are human beings with a purpose to live and experience the beauty and love beyond everyday experiences.

Spiritual healing is nothing magical or superficial. It is rooted in our everyday lives and an everyday, living philosophy. In life we experience suffering in many different ways. We suffer when we want more than we have, we suffer when we feel inferior or even superior, we suffer when we experience highs and lows in life, we suffer when we see the world with dualistic eyes, we suffer when we experience ephemeral phenomenon other than what is, we suffer when we feel our unique beliefs, values, and religion are better and wiser than those of others, and we suffer when we fail to recognize the oneness in diversity.

Spiritual healing teaches us the ways to connect to the cosmos and divinity through our body and experiences, as well as through

Pachamama (mother earth), *Intititi* (father sky), through Jesus, through Buddha, through Krishna, through Allah, and all other connecting agents and instruments. These connecting agents serve the same function and they are neither superior nor inferior to one another. My God is not wiser, more understanding, or better than the God of yours.

Spiritual healing is not about dogmatic rituals we have to perform or specific ways we have to live. It is about the connection to our inner teacher, a teacher who speaks the truth to us when our mind is quiet and there is no interference of learned knowledge or philosophy. It is about our connection to the essences of our universe: water, air, fire, earth and ether. These elements are who we are, where we came from not long ago, and where we will return in the very near future. Spiritual healing is about our connection to our spiritual beings beyond our temporary physical existence in this universe. It is about the connection to the cycle of the universe and the cycle of our human race, cycles that are the same but are viewed differently in the human mind by the creation of time and space.

Difference between Religion and Spirituality

If we go to church every Sunday, does it make us spiritual? If we live in an ashram, does it make us spiritual? If we belong to a religious group, does it make us spiritual? If we read the Bible or spiritual epics, does it make us spiritual? If we believe in God's existence, does it make us spiritual? If we believe in reincarnation, does it make us spiritual? The answers to such questions are not easy for those of us living in this conditioned world, holding a set of beliefs and values based on our culture and education. We have been conditioned on many levels of our existence, both physically and mentally, as well as emotionally and spiritually. Many of us use the terms *religion* and *spirituality* interchangeably as if they had the same meaning, but they do not.

As a matter of fact, religion and spirituality have different meanings at both intellectual and practical levels. Religion is the belief in God, whereas spirituality is the experience with God. Religion sees God above all existence, whereas spirituality sees God as all-encompassing – in you, in me, in everywhere and in everything. Religion assumes superiority over other beliefs, whereas spirituality senses the equality of all existence. Religion teaches that we will be judged and destined to heaven or hell on the date of our death, whereas spirituality sees every moment of our lives as whole and perfect. Religion looks upon God as untouchable, whereas spirituality sees the world as a manifestation of God. Religion views God in a tangible form, whereas spirituality sees God as formless, beyond any boundaries. Religion often teaches that we will be saved by attending church, whereas spirituality sees us living within God in every moment of our lives. Religion uses the word *God* to express God's existence, whereas spirituality uses the word *consciousness* to express God's existence in all manifestations.

Definition of Spiritual Being

A spiritual being is one who lives with harmony, peace, compassion and love. A spiritual being sees unity in world diversity; lives a wholesome, perfect, extraordinary life; sees the world as it is without prejudice or judgment; enjoys every moment as precious; lives with a sense of responsibility and duty; and refrains from engaging in the dramas of the world. The following are characteristics of a spiritual being.

A spiritual being distinguishes the eternal and consistent truth from the ever-changing deception of the false appearances of truth. A spiritual being has a clear perception of reality, feels comfortable with this perception, and is capable of tolerating uncertainty and ambiguity. The uncertainty and ambiguity are seen as opportunities to experience the world, holding open many doors while refraining from placing judgment upon people and events.

A spiritual being accepts oneself as he or she is, and accepts others as they are without judging or evaluating. We all come to this world in a variety of shapes and forms and with different characteristics.

When we no longer place judgments upon ourselves and others, we gain our self-concept and self-worth. When we no longer place our judgments upon others, we are in harmony with all around us.

A spiritual being is spontaneous in both thought and behavior. Spontaneity is to go beyond the tyranny and control of the mind, so we are able to start connecting to the wisdom of the cosmos and the universe. As a result, the innate, creative, spontaneous, pure, childlike, and playful nature becomes who we are in the midst of our world. We become authentic, inventive, expressive, perceptive, and spontaneous in everyday life, and able to see things in new ways in everyday life.

A spiritual being is autonomous, independent of, and a nonconformist to his or her own culture and environment, but does not go against convention for the sake of being different. A spiritual being is confident and content with oneself without conforming to the culture or environment one is immersed in and surrounded by, and one does not feel the need to fulfill the expectations of others, or even his or her own.

A spiritual being is not lonely, even when alone. He or she enjoys and seeks solitude and serenity in mountains, forests, oceans, and even in busy airports. A spiritual being has a mystic or peak experience through meditation, chanting, yoga, singing, playing music, and even playing sports. He or she has had glimpses of the transcendental experience between the literal world and the cosmos.

A spiritual being has feelings of sympathy, affection, love, and compassion for oneself and for others. He or she respects all beings regardless of age, race, creed, and other ephemeral factors, and sees oneness in diversity.

The Experiential Spiritual Health and Healing Lessons

The following lessons are derived from different traditions and serve to bring us harmony within the human race, as well as to bring peace to everyone and to every place. These lessons are experientially oriented, and show ways of revealing the truth within and among us. These lessons may touch us in different ways and on different levels, so it is important to remember that there is no right or wrong connection to these lessons. It is important to understand our own experience in relationship to these lessons as an essential process of spiritual healing. The only criteria we have for the lesson and its experience is to gauge whether we are content, compassionate, happy, and hold love and peace within ourselves and for others.

Each lesson consists of four sections. The first section includes classic stories and personal experiences that touched the heart and life of the author. The second section includes the teaching and shared concepts from different spiritual traditions. The third section presents the ancient wisdom related to the topic. The last section integrates the lesson's theme into everyday life and suggests very specific daily practices.

"Letting Go"
Living a joyful and peaceful life

Story

A traveler came to a great expanse of water and desperately needed to get across. There was no bridge and no ferry, so he built a raft and rowed himself across the river. What should he do with the raft after he crosses the river? Should he decide that because the raft was so helpful to him he should load it onto his back and lug it around with him wherever he goes? The answer is obvious.

Teaching

Many teachings and tools are like the raft, useful to cross the river but not to be held on to and clung to. The sole purpose of any method or tool of spiritual teaching is to enable people to get across the river of pain to the 'other shore', the shore of peace and joy.

In everyday life, we as human beings have the tendency to become attached to things that are familiar to us, and we hold on to the attachments in case we need them for the future because we are afraid of unknowns and unpredictable events. We accumulate lots of 'important junk' in our house, in our possession, and even in our mind. We start repeating the same patterns in life because they are what we know and they are familiar. We wonder why we walk in a circle in life.

'Letting go' goes beyond the metaphorical raft and it teaches us not to hold on to anything that is ephemeral or impermanent. Our material possessions, desires, emotions, thoughts, even knowledge, are bound within time and causation, and are temporary and lead to suffering. Transcending these life phenomena leads to a joyful and peaceful life.

When we learn and craft skills to let go of the things that no longer serve us, let go of the beliefs that prevent us from moving forward, and let go of the possessions that weigh us down, we can start healing our wounds and the past, embarking on our epic journey, and dreaming the world into being.

Ancient Wisdom

The *Yoga Sutras* of Patanjali, ~ 300 B.C.E., Sutra 1.16: Knowing the innermost Self brings supreme non-attachment (*para-vairagya*).

Ultimately, we don't have to do anything to attain detachment but hold on to our meditative practice to reveal the source of all we ever thought we desired. Then there is nothing else to crave; we have found enduring happiness that is there no matter what else appears before us. In the fullness of the heart there is nothing else to desire. In this dispassionate state we enjoy whatever comes to us, and freely release whatever leaves us while attending to *dharma* in the world.

Sutra 1.18: *Para-vairagya* is the practice of indifference to arising thoughts, while absorbed in the unchanging self-luminescence of pure awareness. Over time, *vrittis*, due to lack of interest, simply no longer arise; as a result, we live in natural, persistent inner stillness. This is something we can apply to our own daily meditation – losing interest in whatever disturbs the stillness. This is difficult if we are interested enough in a thought to become involved with it, thus falling back into duality. We have to inspect our interest in arising thoughts and let go of our interest in them. Here we come to true detachment. Letting go of our outer attachments is just practice for the real thing.

Practice

1. Practice 'letting go' of personal material possessions. If any materials of yours are missing, lost, or damaged, can you let them go?

2. Practice 'letting go' of personal attachment to sensual pleasures. If any of your favorite food, entertainment, or even love is missing, can you let it go?

3. Practice 'letting go' of emotions, desires, likes and dislikes. If any of these traits arises in your mind, can you let it go?

4. Practice 'letting go' of our loved ones when they no longer are available in our lives.

Present Moment, Precious Moment
Conscious Breathing

Story

Two monks walked along a riverbank and saw a lady standing on the shore with a basket of food in her arms. The senior monk walked up and asked her, "Why are you standing here?" She replied with tears in her eyes, "When I left this morning and went to the market, there was a bridge here but now it is gone. I cannot get across the river and my children are starving and waiting for my return." The senior monk stepped forward, picked her up, and carried her across the river. The lady went back home and fed her children. The two monks continued their journey to the temple along the riverbank. After a couple of hours of walking they sat down for a rest. The junior monk could not wait any longer and asked, "Father, we took the vow not to touch a woman when we became monks. Why did you carry the woman?" The senior monk answered, "Son, I have left her two hours ago and you are still carrying her."

Teaching

This classic story gives us a profound lesson on how not to carry stuff that no longer serves us, especially the mind's chatters. Many of us can remember the long-lasting suffering and pain from the last break-up, argument, or hardship that happened a long time ago.

Our emotion dwelled in the past holds us back and does not allows us to move forward to experience the creative, unknown, beautiful way of life.

Dwell in the present moment because it is a wonderful moment. The past has already happened and the future is yet to unfold. The present moment is a precious and wonderful moment where the past and the future happen simultaneously – where the past, the present, and the future become one. Oneness only happens when we are in the state of trance, tranquility and creativity.

Many of us have experienced let-downs in life because we thought we would be happy if we got married, bought a big house, and had a good job. There are so many stories in life we have witnessed and personally experienced and we repeat these same stories over and over. The past or the future does not furnish our peace or happiness but only bring us an unchanging state of like and dislike, happy and sad, the duality of the world.

It is a joy to sit at ease and return to our breathing, our smile and our true nature so the essence of our lives can be in the present moment. Peace and joy can be experienced in this moment. If we do not have peace and joy now, do we have to wait for tomorrow or the day after tomorrow?

Ancient Wisdom

Sutra 3.53: By *samyama* on the present moment one can discriminate true knowledge from the false.

Time is not a substantive reality but is only an imaginary concept. We do experience the persistence of the present; however, the concept of time arises from sequences of events built up in memory, thus the abstraction of 'past' arises. Similarly, imaginary constructs of sequences not yet present gives us the unreal 'future'.

Whatever exists in the present is real and true. Whatever appears in the imagination of the past and future is neither real nor true. Deep contemplation of the present allows us to discriminate the true from the false, the real from the unreal.

Time is a quasi-linear, arbitrary measurement of change, and certainly a convenience in physics, music and engineering; however, time is not real – think of it as a shim that makes the math work. You may verify for yourself: in the inner stillness of meditation, what evidence of time do you notice? You will see the only suggestion of time is when words arise related to the concept – and words are imaginary, not real. For example, the word *water* does not quench thirst, and the thought of *light* does not dispel darkness.

Practice

1. Sit quietly, walk gently on the earth, breathe consciously, and talk tentatively so we can experience the precious and wonderful moment.

2. Listen to our breath and the pulsations of the heart and universe because they are manifestations of our precious and wonderful moment.

3. We can practice conscious breathing not only while sitting in a meditation room, but also while working at the office, driving a car, or sitting on a bus. Wherever we are at any time throughout the day, we can follow our breath and we can say simply, "Calming, smiling, present moment, precious moment."

4. As we breathe in, we say to ourselves, "Breathing in, I know that I am breathing in." As we breathe out, we say to ourselves, "Breathing out, I know that I am breathing out." This technique can help focus our mind on our breath. As we practice our breath, will become peaceful and gentle, and our mind and body will also become peaceful and gentle. In a few minutes we can realize the fruit of breath work.

5. We can recite the following four lines as we breathe in and out: "Breathing in, I calm my body. Breathing out, I smile. Dwelling in the present moment, I know this is a precious moment!" This practice is not just for the beginner. Some monks have practiced this for decades.

Surrender to 'What is'
Acceptance of the Now

Story

There was a son and father living in a small village in Japan. They had a horse that helped them plow the field to bring food to the table. One day the horse was gone. A villager came and asked, "How could you live without the horse?" The father replied without emotion, "What is is what is." A few days later the horse came back along with a herd of wild horses. The villager came and said "Wow, you are so lucky. You have so many horses now and you will have a prosperous life ahead of you." The father replied indifferently, "What is is what is." The very next day the son got onto a wild horse and tried to contain her, but fell and broke his arm. The villager came and said, "Poor you! Your family suffers so much and what are you going to do with the wild horses and your life?" The father replied with a smile "What is is what is."

Teaching

To some, surrender may have negative connotations, implying defeat, giving up, failing to rise to the challenges of life, becoming lethargic, and so on. Surrender, however, is entirely opposite. It does not mean to passively do nothing about arising life situations nor does it mean to cease making plans or initiate a plan of action.

Surrender is the simple yet profound wisdom of yielding to, rather than opposing, the flow of life. The only place where you can experience the flow of life is the Now, so to surrender is to accept the present moment unconditionally and without reservation. It is to relinquish inner resistance to what is. Inner resistance is to say "no" to 'what is' through judgment and the conditioned mind. The resistance is the mind. Acceptance of 'what is' immediately frees you from mind identification, and thus reconnects you with being.

It is extraordinarily difficult and arduous to be aware of what is, because our every thought is conditioned and is the projection of our self and it becomes a distraction in pursuing happiness and stillness. We do not understand what is. We look at 'what is' through the spectacles of prejudice, condemnation and identification. In a spiritual sense, surely 'what is' is a fact, the truth, and anything else is an escape and not the truth. To understand what is, the conflict of duality must cease, because the negative response of becoming something other than 'what is' is the denial of the understanding of what is. The understanding of what is and being aware of what is reveals extraordinary depth in which lies reality, happiness and joy.

Ancient Wisdom

Sutra 2.45: *Samadhi* is attained through surrender.

Patanjali is persistent in this theme of surrender. We see that this is the direct path to the highest state of yoga. What does this mean, exactly, to surrender? What do we do, and what state is this? Simply stated, it means for the ego to get out of the way of the silent witness, the conscious indweller. When we look out on the world it is the Self that is seeing and knowing. The ego, with its neediness and fear, has subsided. This is the state of *samadhi*, the culmination of the eight limbs of yoga.

Practice

1. Practice 'surrendering to what is' in your daily life when life situations arise. For example, when we are stuck in a traffic jam, when we are late for a meeting, or when we lose our job.

2. Practice the concepts of 'now, being, what is' without any mind identification, judgment, or prejudice. Learn to recognize the ever-changing nature of our experience in life and start to accept the way presented in front of us without fighting and resistance.

3. Experience 'just being' in everyday life without chatter of the mind when we walk on a trail or a street, when we look at a tree, and when we wake up in the morning.

4. Practice 'letting go' of all expectations in life from within and without. Let go of things that no longer serve us and let go of the egoistic self that has dominated our everyday life.

Power of Thoughts
To control thought is to control our destiny

Story

In the summer of 2005, I led a backcountry outdoor education expedition for a group of college students in Emigrant Wilderness north of Yosemite. The students gathered at a lakefront and socialized for the last time the night before we completed the expedition. They saw a campfire across the lake about a mile away and a few flashing lights moving around and they started pondering what was going on there. Some students were concerned that someone there might be injured and may need assistance, and the students wondered what they should do. Some other students were concerned about these people who may be murderers who come to the wilderness to kill strangers, based on what they read and heard. The disturbance of conversation went on for at least half an hour. They did not know what to do to resolve the issue, and decided to come to my tent to ask me what to do. When I looked out from the tent and saw a campfire and a few flashing lights I told them these people across the lake most likely were fishermen and were enjoying themselves around the campfire. I told them to go back to sleep and not worry about it. It seemed to settle them down but I was told that a couple of female students were too scared to sleep in their own tents so they spent the night with others. The next day on the way home we stopped at a local famous pizza joint, Pie in the Sky, for a treat. I saw a few friends of mine there from back home and asked them what they were doing there. They replied that they had spent a few days at the north end of Relief Lake camping and fishing. I quickly introduced them to my students, "Hey Folks, they were the murderers across the lake from us."

Teaching

The world is the result of a projection of thoughts in the mind. Deep reflection of and philosophical search for the meaning of the world show us that the entire universe is in reality the projection of the human mind. Mind in itself is nothing but a record of impressions that keeps expressing itself ceaselessly as imprints, impulses, or thoughts. Thoughts propel us to act and then actions create fresh impressions in the mind. Through years of practice and inquiries, a yogi checks, controls, and even stops thoughts, the root function of the mind.

Thought exceeds light in speed (186,000 miles/second). Thought travels faster than anything we can measure, such as a moving car, sound or light. There was informal research completed on identical twins; researchers had the twins send each other mental messages telepathically at the end of south and north poles. Interestingly and surprisingly the twins received the messages instantaneously without a delay.

Thought acts as a boomerang. Whatever thoughts we send out of our mind come back to us. Every thought we think is a boomerang. Thoughts of peace sent out by a saint or a wise one travel with lightning speed in all directions and enter the minds of people and produce in them also similar thoughts. Contrarily, a worldly man whose mind is filled with jealousy, revenge and hatred sends out discordant thoughts which enter the minds of thousands and stir in them similar thoughts of hatred and discord. An evil thought has a triple-fold effect. First, it harms the thinker by doing injury to his or her physical and mental body. Second, it harms the person who is the thinker's object. Third, it harms all mankind by polluting the whole mental atmosphere. If we entertain thoughts of hatred, we are really a murderer of that man against whom we foster thoughts of hatred. We are also our own action of suicide, because these thoughts rebound upon us directly.

Thoughts are living objects. Each thought has its energy and vibration. For example, the thought of a bomb and the thought of ocean waves produce a significantly different vibration and action. A single thought of love can illicit chains of thoughts and even emotion. A single thought of our boss produces chains of thoughts about our boss. Whether thoughts are positive or negative, their strength produces energy and a reaction.

Thoughts shape who we are physically, mentally, emotionally and spiritually. 'As we think we become' is another way to express the point. When we think of love we become the love and when we think of joy we become the joy. Thoughts promote radiant health. The body is internally associated with the mind and a gross visible form of the subtle and invisible mind. Mental health is more important than physical health. If the mind is healthy, the body will be healthy. A sound mind results in a sound body.

Every thought produces a strong vibration in every cell of the body and leaves a strong impression there. Every change in thought makes a vibration in its mental body, and this, when transmitted to the physical body, causes activity in the nervous matter of our brain. Man sows a thought and reaps an action. He sows an action and reaps a habit. He sows a habit and reaps a character. He sows a character and reaps a destiny.

Ancient Wisdom

Sutra 1.2: Yoga is the restraint of thoughts in the mind.

The idea is simple: when the mind is restrained to equanimity, the unmoving seer becomes the predominant knower of the mind and its appearance. Once the mind is entrained to contentment by the practice of meditation, the transcendent state gradually persists in our normal awareness in all circumstances. The mind is not different from the thoughts it thinks. Thus: no thought, no mind. The *activity* of yoga is in restraining the mind to equilibrium, and the *state* of yoga is that of the undisturbed seer.

Practice

1. Positive thoughts. Make ourselves positive by taking a positive attitude of the mind consciously, now and then, and it soon becomes habit. When a negative thought or doubt comes into the mind it must be dispelled by well-directed suggestions and affirmations. We will drive off negative thoughts and feelings and will be established in a positive state. The substitution method is very easy and effective in the destruction of negative and even evil thoughts. Cultivate positive, virtuous thoughts of mercy, love, compassion, purity, forgiveness, integrity, generosity and humility in the garden of our own mind.

2. Neutral thoughts. Do not try to drive away negative thoughts. If we do so we will only tax our energy. Instead, feel indifferent and keep quiet because these thoughts will pass soon. Thinking a thought of an ocean, fire, mountain, beach, or creek will resolve the negative thoughts.

3. Embracing thoughts. When thoughts arise in the mind, fully experience the thoughts as they are without judgment. Feel the weight, see the colors, sense the emotion attached to the thoughts, experience the bodily sensations from the thoughts.

4. Spiritual thoughts. The goal of life is the attainment of divine consciousness. If we want to develop thought power to build up our characters and to become great, we will always keep with us some books of inspiring and illuminating thoughts. Repeat Mantras or prayers again and again tentatively. Fill

the mind with divine thoughts and negative thoughts will gradually disappear and vanish.

5. Watching thoughts as an impartial witness. Watch the thoughts passing by like clouds in the blue sky, like wind moving by our skins, like a log drifting away from a river, and like ripples settling down to the calm and tranquil mountain lake. Control the thoughts and be a witness of our own thoughts. Rise above thoughts, watch everything that unfolds in the mind like watching a movie without emotional involvement, and dwell in that pure consciousness where there is no thought.

6. Counting thoughts as they arise. Be aware of thoughts and learn to count thoughts as they arise. This method immediately stops thought process and will most likely, with practice, dispel the thoughts. With practice, not only can we mark our progress to fewer thoughts or even zero thoughts in the mind, but we can also watch the thoughts as an impartial witness and become indifferent to them.

7. Absence of thought can be achieved through yoga synthesis such as concentration, meditation, *pranayama*, *asana*, and all four paths of yoga. Through constant and intense practice of yoga and *sadhana*, spiritual practice, we can reach to the thoughtless and wave-less state of the mind. When we are in that state we actually permeate and pervade every atom of the universe and we start purifying and elevating the whole world. We can attain the state of *jnani*, the wise one, only when we are free from sensual desires and mortal and immoral thoughts. Aloofness and detachment of the body from sensual objects, and aloofness and remoteness of mind from immoral states of mind, are needed for the attainment of *jnani*. Thinking means externalization or objectification. Thinking means differentiation, quality and multiplicity. Thinking is *samsara*. Thinking causes identification with the body. Thinking causes 'I-ness' and

'Mine-ness'. Thinking causes time and space. Stop thinking! Practice 'Stop Thinking' through *vairagya* (dispassion or dis-attachment) and *abhyasa* (persistent practice), and merge ourselves in the Pure Consciousness. When there is no thinking or *sankalpa*, there is the Absolute and the *jivanmukta*, the liberated one.

Mindfulness

Breathe and smile with everything we encounter

Story

The Buddhist monk, Thich Nhat Hanh, led a retreat in Montreal, Canada. He noticed that every time a car stopped in front of him, he saw a few French words on license plates, 'Je me souviens' (I remember). He did not know what was to be remembered but it gave him an idea so he told his audience, "I have a present for all of you here. Every time you see a car stop in front of you with the words 'Je me souviens' you can see it as a bell of mindfulness. It will help remind you to breathe and smile in this very moment. And you will have plenty of opportunities to breathe and smile while driving in Montreal."

One of his friends was delighted and enjoyed the practice in Montreal, but when he came to visit Thich Nhat Hanh in Paris he said that Paris was not a good place to practice mindfulness while driving because there are no signs of 'Je me souviens'. He was instructed to practice mindfulness with red lights and there are plenty of red lights in Paris. When he went back to Montreal he wrote a letter to Thich Nhat Hanh in which he said, "Practicing mindfulness in Paris was pretty easy after all. Not only did I practice with the red lights at the stops signs, but also every time a car stopped in front of me, I saw the eyes of Buddha blinking at me. I had to smile at those blinking eyes."

Teaching

Practicing mindfulness means to bring our awareness to *NOW* and to the present moment in order for us to experience a flower, blue sky, child, tree, or brilliant light. Even when we encounter the real problems in the world, with mindfulness we will know what to do. If we remain aware of mindfulness and continue to practice breathing and smiling, everything in the world (people, animals, plants) will benefit from our ways of conducting ourselves. We actually start planting the seeds for peace and joy on the planet. The teaching and practice of mindfulness, through breathing and awareness of small acts of daily living, heals and transforms difficult psychological states, and leads to personal inner peace and peace on earth.

Being mindful means to be present with whatever we do in everyday life. When we eat, we just eat and enjoy every aspect of the eating experience, the taste and texture of food, without engaging in other activities like reading, watching TV or arguing. When we read, we simply read without engaging in other thoughts and emotions. When we play a sport, we just play the enjoyable and pure aspect of the sport without attaching to the consequences of playing. When we walk, we just walk and enjoy the texture of the ground, the sensations of muscle contractions and the body's reaction to walking, the beauty of passing trees, leaves, flowers, and even blades of grass without trying to figure out what to do with our irritating coworker.

Being mindful is expressed and experienced in a state of single-mindedness. Every task needs our full attention. When we zero in and focus on it, we start to enjoy the process of completing the task. In the process we no longer consider the likes or dislikes of the task. We simply do what we need to do as part of our duties and responsibilities as a father, mother, worker, or teacher.

Ancient Wisdom

Words of the Buddha (from the *Satipatthana Sutta*): What is right mindfulness? There is the case where a monk remains focused on the body in and of itself – ardent, alert, and mindful – putting aside greed and distress with reference to the world. He remains focused on feelings in and of themselves, the mind in and of itself, consciousness in and of itself – ardent, alert, and mindful – putting aside greed and distress with reference to the world. This is called right mindfulness. Right mindfulness leads to the attainment of purity, overcoming of sorrow and lamentation, ending of pain and grief, pursuing of the right path and realization of nirvana.

Right mindfulness is the seventh step of the Buddha's Eightfold Path. The purpose of practicing mindfulness it is to see things as they really are. A key to the experience of mindfulness is the little word "ardent." Ardent means being passionately attentive. We are passionately attentive to the true being of things as they are, so as not to allow the mind to wander into the dream of imagination with its fears and regrets.

Practice

1. Driving. The next time we are diving, pay attention to all details along the road, trees, flowers, colors of cars, shapes of cars, the beauty of the universe. When we are caught in traffic, do not fight; instead, just sit back, smile to yourself, and start enjoying yourself fully with all the beautiful surroundings. We are then in the present moment and can make everyone in the car happy as well.

2. Waking up. When we wake up in the morning, smile. Smile when you take a fresh conscious breath, feeling the cool and invigorating air entering into the body, mind, and soul. Hear birds singing not just with the ears but also the heart, and see beams of light shining through the window, illuminating our body, mind, emotion and soul.

3. Taking the first step of the day. Walking on the Earth is a miracle! Every step we take is a step of rebirth and renewal and a step closer to ultimate spiritual evolution, enlightenment. We do not have to walk in space or on water to experience a miracle. The real miracle is to be awake in the present moment. We can realize the wonder of being alive.

4. Brushing our teeth. Brushing teeth and rinsing the mouth will make our mouth clean and fragrant. Feel the freshness of water and the sensations of brushing and rinsing. The cleanness of mouth reminds to speak purely and lovingly. Do make our words fragrant! Our speech can build world peace, and peace within us in which trust and love can flourish.

5. Meditation. Invite the sound of bell and the joy of being to the body, mind, and soul in perfect oneness, and transcend all anxiety and sorrow into stillness. Body is mindfulness itself, mind entirely free from distraction, and consciousness is revealed in the state of equanimity. Feelings come and go like clouds in a windy blue sky. Conscious breathing is the anchor. Following the breath, breathing in, calming the body, breathing out, smile within. Dwell in the present moment, because this is a wonderful moment.

6. Eating. Turning off the TV, putting down the newspaper, stopping unhealthy conversations, and even stopping all conversations leads to eating consciously and mindfully while enjoying the food and the presence of company. The purpose of eating is not merely to obtain energy, but to eat and feel the divine that dwells in us.

Cosmic and Pure Love
Motiveless tenderness of heart

Story

When I was in India in 2004 I studied with an *ayurvedic* doctor and true *vedantin*, Krishna Murti. He shared one of his experiences with me. One night on the way back to Mysore, after visiting a few villages as a part of his regular selfless service, he was stopped by a couple of crooks and asked to give his money. He gave them the money he collected from the villagers. Then he volunteered to give them his wedding ring and told them that it was worth 5,000 rupees, and he even offered them his clothes and his motorcycle. The two men were stunned and looked at each other; they did not know what to do and asked why he gave his belongs beyond their asking. He replied, "You must have a very difficult life situation and need them more than I do." They were moved and decided not to take any of his belongings and asked him to leave. Dr. Murti started to talk with them and inquired why they were conducting such an act. They said their wives were sick and there was no food on the table for their children. He genuinely offered them jobs at his clinic. They said they did not want to take them because they were afraid he would report them to the police. Later on, one of them took the job and worked for Dr. Murti for a couple of years.

A few days later, after this story, I encountered a situation where a rickshaw driver thought I was stranger in town and took extra miles to get me back to my hotel in order to collect extra money. He asked for 200 rupees. I paid him that amount and gave him an extra 300 rupees. He asked me why. I said to him sincerely, "You must be in need of money because you took an extra effort to get more mileage." He refused to take the extra money and left without looking at me.

Teaching

We human beings are not much different deep inside. Even though our life situations require us to behave accordingly, acting as a thief, robber, crook, saint, or rishi, but the true nature of the human race is pure, sincere, and loving in heart.

What is love for most of us? When we say we love someone, we mean we possess that person, and even legalize the possession. For some reason, when we lose that possession, jealousy, emptiness, and loss arise. Surely such possession is not love. Sentimental and emotional love is not the answer, because it is merely a form of self-expansion and sensations derived from the thoughts in the mind. A sentimental and emotional person can be stirred to opposite characters of love such as hatred, jealousy, and even murder. Sympathy, forgiveness, possessiveness, jealousy, and fear are all not love. They are fantasy in the mind. The mind corrupts love, and it cannot give birth to love. When all of these have stopped, the pure love comes into existence.

The person with pure love obviously has no enmity to all these characters and he is indifferent. Pure love is revealed only when there is no possession, no envy, and no greed and when there is respect, mercy, and compassion in the stillness of mind.

Pure love is love without attachment, expectation, and desire. It comes from within and is our true nature, and who we are indeed. Love disregards all of the differences of our forms, names, beliefs, values, culture, race, and religion. Love is nothing but the tenderness of our loving heart that shines light to everyone and every place.

Ancient Wisdom

Verse 11 in "Chamakam" of *Sri Rudram*: I will think only sweet and beneficial thoughts. I will do only sweet actions. I will select sweet things to offer in worship. I will always speak sweetly to both gods and human beings. May the gods protect me from any faults in what I say and make my speech graceful.

The *Rudram* is from the *Tattiriya Samhita*, one of the most revered books of the *vedic* literature. The *Rudram* is a sacred chant of the Saraswati Order of Monks, chanted every day in ashrams and monasteries reflecting the highest qualities of every human being. When we recognize this sweetness as our essential Self, then we know the Divine Love that we are.

Practice

1. Cultivate pure love without motive through the daily *sadhana* or spiritual practice including *asana*, meditation, *pranayama*, selfless service, devotion to the supreme power, and self inquiry of "Who am I?"

2. Provide the motiveless tenderness of love to yourself, friends, family members and even difficult people in your life. Love yourself for who you are and love others for who they are.

3. Record the events and inner experience in a journal when you provide pure loving thoughts and acts to others without attaching to the fruits of the thoughts and acts.

4. Love all beings in the universe, trees, animals, earth, sky, rocks, rivers, mountains, fires, earthquakes and even murderers unconditionally. It would be a very challenging task but yet a transcending experience from mortality to immortality.

Who Am I?

Roar like a lion, not bleat like a sheep

Story

Once, a baby lion was born in the forest and his parents left him behind. A clan of sheep rescued him and raised him along with the rest of the sheep. He learned how to select edible plants to eat, how to communicate with others, and even how to escape from danger like the rest of the sheep. He became the sheep lion. One day a big mom lion approached the clan of sheep and they all started running away for their life, including the sheep lion. The mom lion was perplexed when she saw a lion running along with the sheep, so she caught up with the sheep lion and asked, "Why are you running away?" "Bleat, bleat, bleat, I am afraid you will eat me," answered the sheep lion. The mom lion could not stop laughing and even became more confused. So she asked, "Why are you talking like a sheep and acting like a sheep?" "I am a sheep," bleated again the sheep lion. "Come with me. I shall show you who you are," the mom lion requested. She took the sheep lion to a lake and said to the sheep lion, "Look at yourself in the lake and tell me who you are." The sheep lion was hesitant to look at the lake but eventually he did. He saw himself just like the lion standing next to him and he was awakened. So he roared in the air, "I am a lion" and went on as a lion into the forest.

Teaching

Who are we truly? Are we a father, mother, son, daughter, teacher, husband, wife, politician, or employee? We have been conditioned to be a role and we play a combination of roles as a reflection of the society, culture, race, politics, and environment that shape who we are. We have lived in this paradigm for centuries, and few of us have recognized who we truly are without the veils of the conditioned mind. Therefore we keep looking for something else in life, but life seems to have failed us every time.

We find who we are when we lift the veil of the conditioned mind and *samskara*, and we experience the essence of our existence. We all experience a glimmer of pure joy, love, and contentment in our life when the mind, body, and the world are in complete stillness. There are no thoughts, no mind, no likes or dislikes, and no story, just being, being here and now.

How can we get to that state and how can we lift all the veils in our lives to reveal our true selves? It is not an easy process to reach destiny, but a joyful journey to experience it.

Ancient Wisdom

Yoga Vasistha, written by Valmiki around 2000 B.C.E.: What is inquiry? To inquire thus: "Who am I?" is true inquiry. Knowledge of truth arises from such inquiry; from such knowledge there follows tranquility in oneself; and then there arises the supreme peace that passeth understanding, and the ending of all sorrow. *Vicara*, or inquiry, is neither reasoning nor analysis: it is directly looking into oneself.

At the core of this text the author suggests that self-inquiry is the essential practice to purify the mind. Then, in this pure state of meditation we know that our innermost identity is the Universal Consciousness that manifests in our life as the sweetness of peace and bliss.

Practice

1. Learn to let go of mind-made emotion, stress, anxiety and duality of the world. You know they are not your true self.

2. Learn to love others and enjoy others just like yourself.

3. Learn to experience the true self through the stillness derived from meditation, *asana* and *sadhana* practice.

4. Use the meditation method of "Who Am I" to peel each layer of veils. For example, when a thought about your job comes to your mind, you simply answer to yourself, "I am not employee. I am not employee." Then ask yourself again, "Who am I?" and continue to meditate and self-inquire.

Meaning of Life

Experience and liberation from experience – a journey, not a destination

Story

I was inspired to share this story with you when I watched a movie entitled *Peaceful Warrior* in Berkeley with a group of yogis in the summer of 2006. One day the coach, a spiritual master, told a student he had something important to show him and believed he was ready to receive the special gift. They walked and hiked together to a mountaintop with joy and happiness. They talked and chatted about everything they encountered and observed. When they got to the top of the mountain, the student asked what it is the secret gift was, besides the scenic view. The master told him it is right under his foot. "A rock?" wondered the student. "Yes, the ordinary rock. I did not know what we would find at the destination." Then the student picked up the rock and recited to himself a resonance to his master's teaching. Life is a journey, not a destination. Life is experience and liberation from experience.

Teaching

We live in the world performing the roles of teachers, engineers, doctors, philosophers, fathers, mothers, students, etc. The role we play brings us satisfaction and dissatisfaction, likes and dislikes, and enjoyment and sufferings. So we constantly look for something else to do and to become someone we are not at this moment. We chase one dream after another. The end result seems to repeat itself. We wonder why and do not realize our conditioned minds tend to perform the familiar pattern over and over. We are caught in the cycle of *samskara* (behavior tendencies) and the past. We anticipate what will be happening in the unknown future, and expect something bound to happen to bring us power, wealth, and love. The duality of roles we play fails to provide us contentment and eternal happiness and joy.

We shall dream the world into being like a child playing on the beach, building a beautiful sand castle, day-dreaming the future and/or the past, and indulging in so-called trivial tasks perceived by adults. We have forgotten that innocent part of ourselves when we got educated and fully immersed into our contemporary culture as we grew up. The conditioned mind took over our intuitive mind and we then lost our connection to our own souls and the soul of universe, which in turn has distorted our inner purpose of life.

Experience in life and liberation from experience teaches us that life is a journey, not a destination. To experience every moment of our day, every task at hand, and every role we play brings us to here and now, the true existence of the human race. No more past to dwell on and no more future to worry about. It is then that we come to being, manifested in the state of bliss and joy.

Ancient Wisdom

At end of this life journey, what have we truly accomplished? The ancient *Katha Upanishad* tells us: As one draws the pith from a reed, so must the aspirant after truth, with great perseverance, separate the Self from the body. Know the Self to be pure and immortal.

Practically speaking, these human creatures are a two-in-one apparatus. We have the physical, created from stardust, and the non-physical, uncreated, infinite, intelligent knower of the objective creation. It is the conscious indweller that enlivens the physical host. Without the conscious indweller, the host quickly decays.

At some point in time this two-in-one apparatus will separate. So, which will go where? It is evident that the stardust physical form will decay and may someday become part of another form. It is also evident that the uncreated and undying consciousness of the indweller will not decay but will merge with Universal Consciousness. That which is truly you will continue in awareness.

But what happens to the mind, memory and identity: the illusory ego conjured by consciousness and applied to the body? Does it retain its identity in the astral realm? Nothing that is created follows the uncreated. Just as matter is a creation in the physical universe, thought, memory and identity are created in the mental universe. Thus the mind falls away with the body at the end of this turbulent association with Spirit.

It is incumbent upon us to learn the teaching of the *Katha Upanishad* and, while still in the body, discriminate the separateness of the Self from the body. We do this through the practice of meditation in which the Self becomes aware of itself, where we experience the joyous serenity of our true nature. Then we are free.

Practice

1. Consciously observe every thought, action, task, duty, and role you play and experience them fully and try to spiritualize them in the light of acceptance, surrender, and embracement.

2. Continue self-inquiry and ask, "Who am I?" and answer the question with, "*Neti neti*" – "I am not this I am not that" – until your immortal Self reveals.

3. Keep a daily journal on your spiritual journey to reflect the transforming experience and the identity shift, from mortal self to immortal Self.

4. Continue searching for our destiny and balance in daily life and the inner journey.

5. Dare to "travel far but be sure to come back" – remember always to come back to our body to experience who we are as human beings, no matter how far we are traveling in our literal life or esoteric journey.

Active Listening – an Act of Generosity
Dialogical inquiry as a spiritual health practice

Story

One day I paid a visit to my friend's family. I started playing with their two-year-old daughter. "Uncle Ping, let's do yoga" said she. So we did cat pose, cobra pose, candles pose, bow pose, and other poses together. "We are going to learn a new pose today called down dog," I said to her. "Now follow me, putting your hands on the floor, keep your leg straight, push your hip up to the sky." She followed me perfectly. Then I said, "Follow me and lift one leg up behind you, like dog pee-pee." The next day her Mom told me what happened that night before she went to bed. "Mommy, let me show you a new yoga pose, dog pee-pee," and there she went, a perfect down dog pose with one leg up in the air, and then she actually peed on the floor...

Teaching

Active listening in dialogue form is an act of generosity, in which we human beings offer our full presence and attention to another fellow human being. In dialogue, participants are encouraged to suspend their assumptions, values and beliefs and explore them together in playful and non-confrontational ways. There is no agenda, but awareness of the context in which ideas are spawned and creative alternatives are explored. When we are able to maintain mindful dialogue and passionately argue for what we consider to be true at any given time with humbleness and non-attachment, then we can recapture the critical force of dialogue, while preventing the conversation from becoming a battle.

In dialogical inquiry, the virtues of generosity can be revealed through the practice of active listening and conscious and mindful speech. Active listening means paying attention to another human being from the start to the end without entanglement in our own mind with identification and interpretation. By doing so we do not miss or distort what others are trying to say. Active listening cultivates the skill of not only paying attention to linguistic content but also to the whole being. The critical element of active listening, however, is the inner listening or direct knowing, that is, the anchoring of our consciousness in ourselves while giving our attention to another person.

Conscious and mindful speech is used to express our ideas in the spirit of truthfulness and compassion with force and clarity, even if it may involve taking risks or overcoming fears.

Ancient Wisdom

Sutra 3.34: *Siddhis* may also be attained through *pratibha* (inner listening), thus knowledge of everything arises spontaneously.

Everyone has an occasional flash of intuition – direct knowing beyond any rational deduction. As the student of yoga deepens in meditation, the inner light of wisdom flashes more frequently, but we must learn how to discriminate insight from rational thought. Through persistence in *sadhana*, inner stillness will predominate in the inner landscape and the flow of intuition will increase. Gradually the light of *pratibha* becomes a continuous stream and we can shine this light of wisdom upon all matters.

How do we do this? What attitude must prevail for *pratibha* to persist as steady wisdom? Notice that at any given moment we are listening to the prattle in the mind. Not that there is anything of redeeming value in the mind, but the fact is we are listening. This is something we know how to do already. In the stillness of meditation we turn our awareness to listening beyond the emptiness. By focusing our listening deep into the boundless infinite we open a conscious channel to the light of wisdom. The shift is subtle, yet profound. See what your experience is while listening in on the stillness beyond the mind. We draw inspiration from consciousness itself.

Practice

1. Mindfulness – The practice of mindfulness in our daily life involves observing our own consciousness, thoughts, emotions, and body sensations as well as being aware of all these dimensions of conversation with a dialogical partner. The quality of this attention is non-judgmental, open, curious, receptive, and appreciative.

2. Surrender – Regardless of whether we agree or disagree with an expressed view, practice accepting all contributions unconditionally. Keep in mind, when we express ourselves we shall disclose openness and honesty and display vulnerability to criticism so that all contributions are valued and respected.

3. Selfless Service – To be at service of something greater than our own personal and egocentric agenda is a transpersonal motivation crucial for developing non-attachment to our views. To one, a thing may be the search for truth, to others the expression of truthfulness and the collective flow of ideas, or the search for liberation from the world of *maya*.

4. Non-attachment – The art of dialogical inquiry is to practice non-attachment to our own ideas, beliefs, and values. It is fundamental to be aware that we are not our thoughts, beliefs and values, and they are only required though our conditioned mind and experience. We do not need to identify

with them. To practice non-attachment allows us to explore our ideas in more playful and relaxed ways and allows us to open unlimited possibilities for constructive transformation of ourselves and our lives.

5. Transformation and Liberation – The uncovering of assumptions, beliefs and values, at personal and interpersonal levels, can help us to transform limiting views about ourselves and the world around us. At the spiritual level, spiritual insights and literature, and even the final liberation from the world, occurs in the conversational or interpersonal context.

Flow into Life

Do not look at the turbulence, go with the flow of the river

Story

In Summer 2006, my dear yogi comrades, Bryan and Josephine, and I led a canoe yoga retreat for 12 days on Noorie River in Quebec, Canada. It was the first canoe expedition I had ever taken. I canoed here and there around lakes and flat waters in the past and never imagined myself running a canoe through class one, class two, even class three rapids. I was struggling at the beginning. When I approached a rapid, even just a class one rapid, I noticed my muscles tense up, my heart beat faster, my acute stress level elevated, my eyes fixed on the white water rapids, my ears filled with the roaring thunder of water, my mind entangled with worlds of thoughts of fear, failure, excitement, and determination and the expectation to succeed. The canoe felt like it bumped into every wave in the river. Well, you know what happened? I fell out of the boat at the class three rapid as a classic example and floated down the river feeling like my bottom hit every rock in the river. Then one day, right before we approached another class three rapid, Bryan told us, "Do not look at the turbulence; go with the flow of the river." Here I went, my canoe and I soared through the rapid with ease, peace, and tranquility while all the noise of the world and the mind subsided. No More Turbulence, No More Waves, and No More Noise, Just the Flow of the River, the Flow of Magical Energy, the Flow of Inner Being.

Teaching

The river is our life path, turbulence or rapids are the life situations, and the noises of the external and internal world are the perception of our mind, awareness and consciousness. What do we do in dealing with life situations? We fall right into the rapids, the dramas of our life. We get entangled with the dramas of the world and feel every bit of turbulence from outside and from within. We fell stressed, depressed, desperate, and even confused about the meaning of life. Even when we get out of drama and feel release, pleasure, and happiness, we quickly fall right back into another drama of our life. The cycle of *samskara* – the conditioned mind and behaviors – continues unless:

> We start disassociating with and being dispassionate about our dramas and become aware of the flow of life;

> We start aligning the inner life path with our the outer life;

> We start listening to the 'inner voice of being' when the mind is tranquil and still;

> We start cultivating pure love and peace within, giving to ourselves and the world around us; and

> There is less and less turbulence in our life.

Ancient Wisdom

Tao Te Ching by Lao Tzu – 600 B.C.E., verse 48: By letting go, it all gets done; The world is won by those who let it go! But when you try and try, The world is beyond winning.

The philosophy of Lao Tzu is simple: accept what is in front of you without wanting the situation to be other than it is. Study the natural order of things and work with it rather than against it, for to try to change 'what is' only creates resistance.

Practice

1. Every morning when you get up and feel the freshness of body and quiet peacefulness of mind, try to bring the sweetness of mind to the world you are about to enter again.

2. Take a few minutes or longer to sit quietly or meditate and feel peacefulness flowing into your heart and your world around you.

3. Practice listening and being consciousness of inner intuition to guide your action when falling into life's dramas.

4. Practice being an impartial witness of dramas and watch them unfold without fueling the energy to the fire of dramas.

Action in Inaction and Inaction in Action
Do not be a doer, but be the Conscious Indweller

Story

A few years back when I started teaching yoga I remembered vividly that I was so happy to see so many students in my yoga class. Then one day there were only a few students that showed up. I was so agitated and unhappy and started to analyze what happened. Was it because the students did not like my teaching style, did not like the yoga style, did not like what I said, did not like… I felt awful at the end of class. It is obvious that my ego was affecting the experience with all the dramas unfolding in my mind while I was trying to conduct the class.

Teaching

How do you conduct a yoga class or do a task in life without affecting the state of mind? One way to answer the question is not to identify your ego self as a doer. Rather, identify yourself as the conscious indweller, a watcher of the doer, who observes the life situations unfold without getting the ego entangled. We do whatever comes to us with full attention and appropriate action. It may mean to use our mental capacity, physical capability, and intellectual creativity to resolve a problem or successfully complete a task, but at the same time, the mind is rooted and established in the state of peace and without attachment to the consequences of the action. You are at peace regardless of how complicated and heated the life situation is that you may encounter. Now you are in the state of Action in Inaction.

Another way to answer the question is to think of yourself as a conduit or an instrument wherein the action, or the doer, happened to flow through you. You simply pass down the knowledge or teaching to others without identifying yourself as the doer. You are at ease and peace while you perform a series of actions without attachment to the fruit of the actions. Now you are in the state of Action in Inaction.

Using yogic tools to still the mind and to establish equanimity before conducting a task or yoga class is another answer. Experience the flow of tranquil state into the action. Now you are firmly established in peace within, regardless of what happens outside. Your inner peaceful and joyful state, which is your birthright, is not affected. Now you are in the state of Inaction in Action.

Ancient Wisdom

Yoga Vasistha, V:13: Rooted in equanimity, doing whatever happens to be the appropriate action in each given situation and not ever thinking about what has thus befallen you unsought, live non-volitionally – doing yet not doing what has to be done.

What's the point in this practice? It's only the ego that thinks it is the doer. It is also just the ego that has expectations about the outcome of action. We bring much suffering upon ourselves through attachment to outcome; it is a source of disappointment and anger in our lives. No expectation, no ego. No ego, no doer. No doer, only inner peace.

Practice

1. Learn to watch every action you take in your daily life and experience it as an impartial witness of the action.

2. Learn to watch every thought and emotion arise, not letting the thought and emotion taking you into a deep rabbit hole or a turbulent rapid. Just simply experience the sensations derived from thoughts and emotions.

3. Learn to complete a task or resolve a problem while the mind is in the state of complete peace.

4. Learn to practice performing an action without attaching to the fruits of the action.

5. Learn to trust your intuition and use the intuition to find a solution to resolve a problem in life by quieting the mind through meditation or other forms of yoga and, as a result, experience the fruit of practicing "Inaction in Action."

6. Contemplate the concept 'Action in Inaction and Inaction in Action' and apply it to your everyday life.

Experiential Embodiment
A genuine source of Inner Stillness

Story

Inhale, stride one-two-three, exhale, stride one-two-three, inhale, stride one-two-three exhale, stride one-two-three… The leg muscles found the sense of rhythm, the lungs regulated their breathing rhythm, the heart sunk in rhythmic dance, the mind fell into a flow of trance, everything that happened within and around became a slow motion picture. I am in the zone, in the flow, or in the state of joy, peace, contentment, and inner stillness.

Teaching

Have you had that experience or a glimpse of that experience through running, hiking, yoga, tai chi, playing a musical instrument, painting, listening to music, or any type of physical exertion? In this experience there was no thought and emotion, but a deep sensation of bodily awareness and a sense of dis-embodiment. I bet we all have had that experience, even if we were not aware of it. This sensation emerges from creative inner-play of both immanent and transcendent spiritual energy in individuals who embrace the fullness of human experience while remaining firmly grounded in body and earth.

Experiential embodiment views all human dimensions, physical body, senses or vital world, heart, emotion, and mind as equal contributors to bring the self and the surrounding world into full alignment with universal consciousness, out of which everything arises. For example, when a celibate monk sublimates sexual desire to increase the devotional love of the heart, when a tantric practitioner uses sexual energy as fuel to transcend bodily sensations into dis-embodiment or trans-human states of being, when an elite athlete transcends bodily and emotional sensations into "zone" performance, or when an artist transcends all facets of human noise into a creative piece of art…

Experiential embodiment regards the body as a subject, a living world, a complete human being that life leads to the ultimate reunion of humanity and universal consciousness in the body. The body is a source of universal consciousness, not given in the form of any metaphysical vision, but gracefully granted through states of being that render and transcend naturally meaningful and profound life experiences. The body is a microcosm of universal consciousness, within which is contained the innermost structure of human transformational experience. Through the bodily experience, the body becomes the psychosomatic organism that is calmly alert, without the intentionality of the mind, and it becomes the conscious awakening of every cell of the organism. Through the bodily experience, the body becomes permeable to both immanent and transcendental reality, and it becomes the truth that has found its own yoga, so to speak, through rhythm, habits, postures, movements, and charismatic rituals.

When the body is felt as our home for awakening, the natural world becomes the landscape of our homeland. Nature is discerned as an organic embodiment of the universal consciousness and as intrinsically sacred, offering natural resources for ecologically grounded yogic life that overcomes the spiritual alienation often manifested as "floating anxiety." When our somatic or physical body and sensations of the vital world are invited to take part in the consciousness awakening, the body and mind become sacred and become conduits to experience consciousness evolution. The more human dimensions actively participating in process of consciousness awakening and liberation, the more channels are tuned into and become the sources of evolution. In short, a complete human being is firmly grounded within consciousness, is fully open to liberation, and is in transformative communion within that consciousness. This is Experiential Embodiment, using the body as an instrument to experience the state of consciousness.

Ancient Wisdom

The *Pratyabhijna-hridayam*, eleventh century tantric text, by the Kashmiri sage Kshemaraja, Sutra 4: Even the individual, whose nature is Consciousness in a contracted state, embodies the universe in a contracted form.

In his commentary on this sutra, Swami Shantananda tells us: "The capacity for full Self-realization – knowledge of our fullness and perfection – is within us in this very moment. Everything we are to become exists within us and is completely available to us right now – it is only a question of our perception."

It is clear from this that we can know fullness and perfection within us as a conscious indweller. We do this through purification of mind, attaining the inner stillness through which this perfection is revealed.

Practice

1. Train your mind to recognize sensations that arise from the body and mind, and make sure to fully experience and explore the sensations.

2. When you practice yoga or other types of physical embodiment, be aware of bodily sensations and open your heart to the experience beyond the sensations once the mind becomes calm and quiet.

3. Use the natural world as a source of embodiment, and sense everything that derives from your interaction with nature; for example, while you are walking in the woods or even on a street.

4. Use all dimensions of the senses to experientially embody and live with the sensations.

Form and Formlessness
A balance of Spiritual and Dharmic life

Story

Once I had a vivid "dream," or you may call it a near-death experience. My heart was beating so fast that I felt I was having a heart attack; my breathing was so heavy and shallow that I was gasping for thin air to survive, my body felt like boiling water pouring out to my skin. I started stumbling over and barely managed to find a place to sit down and asked a bystander, "Please call 911, I am dying…" I remember that I was asked for health insurance and had to be taken to an ambulance. By then I had disconnected from the world. But from my recollection, I remember that I saw people randomly show up in front of me and say goodbye, then leave. They included some family members, some friends, and some others I had never seen before. Then my body became dust and wind and started blowing into the desert, forest, sea … what a release! … then I saw a human wearing a white coat walking towards me. "Am I alive?" I asked. "Barely, but you are now," said the doctor who stood next to me.

Teaching

Have you had an out-of-body experience where all the forms were dissolved into formlessness? It does not necessary have to be a dramatic experience like mine. It may occur any time within any event in our lives when the form is no longer identified and all the noises of the mind and the world are subsided. One becomes a part of the clouds, a part of the animals that hide in the ravines, a part of the water, dust, and wind that come from the earth. One becomes a part of everything and becomes a soul of the universe and a conscious indweller.

Form is the projection of the conditioned mind, where it is contracted with past experiences or the past lives (*samskara*). Because the form is conditioned it changes over a period of time. It stays impermanent. For example, a beautiful castle seems that it keeps its form for a long time but over a short period of a million years, when we consider the creation of universe, it crumbles and dissolves into dirt and dust, formless.

Formlessness, however, is permanent, eternal and oneness. The experience we have is always the same when we enter the realm of the formless and when we experience the state of stillness. The universe and we become one where peace, love, joy, and contentment permeate through the forms.

If what we found were matter or form it would mean nothing in the pursuit of our life's journey, but what we find instead is a moment of light greater than the explosion of a star, and it will never spoil nor disappear. The existence of this world is simply evidence that there exists a world that is perfect with and without form. The world is created by universal consciousness so that, through visible objects and conditioned thought forms, we understand the spiritual teachings, the marvel of wisdom, and the experience of oneness behind the veil of forms. We immerse ourselves into all forms and names on the face of the earth, which gives us an understanding of the world. We do not even have to go to a desert to understand the desert. All you have to do is contemplate a simple grain of sand and to see in it all the marvels of creation.

Ancient Wisdom

Yoga Vasistha, V:40 (Vishnu to Prahlada): Even though you are in the body, since you do not have the body, you are bodiless, formless. You are the observer which is immaterial intelligence: just as, though air exists in space it is not attached to space, and hence it is free from spatial limitation.

Valmiki tells the mythical story of Vishnu teaching Prahlada. In this metaphor, Vishnu represents the Inner Self, whereas Prahlada is a person attached to and identified with the ego and the body. Similarly, our mind learns of the formless Self through stillness in meditation and has the experience of formlessness, not attached to the body. This is the most sublime practice of *vairagya*, non-attachment.

Practice

1. Listen to the sound of a bell, or any sound. Identify yourself with the vibration of the sound, and dissolve yourself into silent formlessness when the sound disappears.

2. Look at a tree, a flower, or a piece of furniture without identifying in the conditioned mind as a form, and experience the light and stillness shining through it.

3. Experience the stillness or formlessness amidst all the busy work, duties, jobs, and responsibilities in the world.

4. Listen to your heart or "direct knowing" when your mind is quiet without form. It knows all things because it came from the soul of the world and it will one day return there.

5. Spiritualize every moment of the day from form to formless and then from formless to form so our spiritual life and *dharmic* life are balanced.

Stillness Amidst the World
Be a Peaceful Warrior

Story

Many of us have watched the film *Forest Gump*. Forest served in the Army in the Vietnam War, saved lives and was a war hero. He was a world-class table tennis player and a true national hero. He was a successful entrepreneur in the shrimp business and was admired by others. One day he decided to run, so he kept on running until he decided not to run any more... He simply followed his life *dharma*, followed his duties and responsibilities without identifying the ego self as the doer. He did what flowed into his life naturally and did so with full attention, heart and enthusiasm. He immersed himself into deep stillness amidst the world dramas and turbulences. He lived in the world as an enlightened being without knowing it.

Teaching

Can we live like Forest Gump who experienced stillness and peace while fully participating in world events? Can we live like Forest Gump who successfully and enthusiastically engaged in his duties and his inner callings while maintaining stillness without ego identification? Can we live like Forest Gump who never wants to become someone else but followed his intuition and personal legend?

Can we live like Forest Gump who lived in the present moment, not attached to the fruits of his actions?

Establishing ourselves in stillness is the answer for these questions. So what is stillness? Stillness can be described as a state of being without disturbances. It can be perceived when we encounter objects and subjects at one level, while at another level it can flow into action in our lives where tasks and work are carried out.

When we first see an object like a tree, flower, car, or even a person, there is a moment of stillness. Then we become lost into thought-forms when we start immediately identifying the object with the conditioned mind and start labeling the object, 'autumn tree', 'colorful tree', 'It would be great to have the tree in my backyard', 'flower smells like chocolate', 'shapes like butterfly', 'look like dying', 'strange cloth', 'fat', 'white', 'sad', 'serious', 'happy', and 'calm'. The phenomenon becomes form in which it loses its aliveness, energy, being, and the stillness.

When a form is dissolving and disappearing, the form becomes formless – the state of stillness. For examples, at the end of a bell ring, at the end of exhalation, at the end of a yoga class, and at the end of our lives, we experience the stillness and consciousness in formlessness.

We also see stillness in others as a reflection of who we are. When we go behind the mind and body identification, there is oneness which resides in all of us. If we recognize our psychological conditioning is transparent, we find the stillness in everything we do and every drama we encounter and we can transcend names, forms, labels, dramas, and actions.

Ancient Wisdom

Sutra 1.12: Thoughts in the mind are restrained by practice (*abhyasa*) and non-attachment (*vairagya*).

In the path of yoga, *sthiti* (steadiness of mind) is a very important concept. We attain *sthiti* through practice (*abhyasa*). A contemporary Siddha master said, "Meditation is to attain the steady state." In this steady state we are undisturbed by the dramatic excesses of the world. We are utterly centered in equipoise. This centeredness is obviously the very opposite of tyranny of the mind.

Sutra 1.13: Of these two, effort toward steadiness of mind is practice.

Patanjali begins the *Yoga Sutras* by saying the state of yoga is attained by restraining the mind to equilibrium. Now he tells us how: devoted practice and detachment. Very simple... there are only two things to do: meditate every day and cultivate selfless dispassion.

Practice

1. Experience the stillness when you first encounter an object, and try to stay with the stillness for as long as you can without identifying the object with the mind.

2. Experience the stillness at the end of any form, such as a dying flower, the end of a gathering, the end of a breath, the end of life, etc.

3. Experience the stillness amidst all the busy work, duties, jobs, and responsibilities in the world.

4. Experience the stillness in others by not labeling them.

The All-Pervading Spirit of Satyagraha
Experiments with Truth

Story

During World War II in Nazi Germany, a Jewish man, seeking refuge from an uncertain future, went to a farmhouse of a German who happened to be a yogi. He asked the German, "May I stay in your house and will you hide me?" "Of course," the German replied without hesitation. The German made a small apartment in his basement and provided the Jew with all the necessary supplies. Days later, a Nazi officer knocked at the door and asked, "Are there any Jews in this house?" The farmer yogi knew truth must always be in harmony with *ahimsa* (non-violence) in thought, action, and deed. Therefore, his impeccable response was "No, there are no Jews in this house."

Teaching

Did the Farmer Yogi not tell the truth about hiding a Jew in his house? By declaring the presence of the Jew, he would be committing an act of violence, not only against the Jew, but against the Nazi officer and himself as well because he would become implicated in the injury. If he answered, "Yes," he knew intuitively he would violate the precept of *ahimsa*. Truth, therefore, in order to merit the support of thought, words, and actions, must be in harmony with *ahimsa*. Gandhi wrote in his autobiography that a perfect vision of truth can only be followed by a complete realization of *ahimsa*.

There are three levels of truth: relative truth, *ahimsa* truth, and cosmic truth. In our culture, it seems that almost everyone believes he or she has a corner on what is the truth. Ask the person on the opposite end of an argument, listen to a talk show host, or watch TV commentators. All claim to know the truth. A so-called truth can only be considered a relatively true fact, which changes every second and never stays permanent.

Truth is not only truthfulness in word, but also truthfulness in thought, action and deed. Truth is not only the relative truth of our conception, but also the absolute truth, the eternal principle. To see the universal and all-pervading Spirit of Truth face to face, one must love all creations in the world as oneself. There is only one absolute truth, *sat-chit-ananda*, all-pervading existence, knowledge, and absolute bliss, within and without. There is only one truth without a second. The absolute truth realizes the unity in diversity and realizes the absolute reality within.

Identification with truth is impossible without self-purification. Without self-purification, the observance of the absolute truth and the law of *ahimsa* remains an empty dream. Self-purification must apply to all walks of life. Purification of oneself leads to the purification of one's surroundings. To attain the perfect purity one has to become absolutely passion-free in thought, speech, and action, to rise above the opposing currents of love and hatred, attachment and repulsion. Yoga teaches us to think, speak, and act in service to the *ahimsa* truth and the absolute truth at all times, in all places, and in all circumstances. Any disharmony with *ahimsa* and divine absolute truth is an opportunity for renunciation. You can only know the truth by experiencing the truth, and you can experience the truth only by letting go of all conditioned forms and names that lead to your belief.

Ancient Wisdom

Sutra 2.35: When one is established in harmlessness (*ahimsa*), those near are at peace.

The virtue of *ahimsa* is born in meditation. When one becomes established in undisturbed inner peace then harmlessness is practiced effortlessly in the world. Not only is the yogi undisturbed by provocation, but the state itself is a calming force that shines in one's company.

Sutra 2.36: When the yogi is firmly established in truth (*satya*), the power of fruitful action is acquired.

One grounded in truthfulness gains will-power and potency of thought and speech. Not only what one says is true, but what one says becomes true. It becomes so through no action. Even though willful, *satya* transcends *karma*.

Practice

1. Examine a so-called truth you hold during a conversation or an argument, analyze its impermanency, or the fact of its relative truthfulness, and then question why you decide to hold on to that truth.

2. Experience the difference between relative truth and divine absolute truth.

3. Apply *ahimsa* into your speech, thoughts, and action in the search of the absolute truth.

4. Experiment with the *ahimsa* truth and absolute truth in everyday life, at work, at home, in conversation, and even in most aversive situations.

Listen to the Inner Voice
The practice of Spontaneous Direct Knowing

Story

One day I was driving northbound on Highway 99 while trying to decide where to go for the weekend, San Francisco or Grass Valley. I attempted to rationalize my decision with my reasoning mind, listed pros and cons for both destinations, but failed to come closer to a conclusion. So I decided to let go of the reasoning process and just to listen to the inner voice without engaging my mind. I quieted my mind and started gazing out through the window into the silence and stillness of trees, traffic lights, and darkness of the sky. Unfortunately, there was still no answer as I was getting close to the exit to San Francisco. I stayed in the lane right next to the exit in case I needed to exit. At the very moment of exiting I felt an impulse that propelled me to stay on the course. As I passed the exit, I curiously glimpsed at the exit lane to see if I could exit but there was a car adjacent to my car so that I would not be able to exit anyway. I broke into a smile, laugh, and joy…

Teaching

We all have on occasion spontaneously experienced accurate intuitive knowing. The phone rings, for example, and we know who it is. Or we think of someone we have not seen or heard from for a long time, and then receive a card or bump into that person on the street the next day. We know what someone is going to say, and then he or she says it. Many coincidences happen that are intuitively foreseen.

Direct knowing is the means of appropriate or so-called "right" action, and it is the deepest knowing made conscious. It is the universal language which communicates truth about the way things are. It involves listening inwardly for communication from the universe. It answers questions consciously concerning who we are and how the world works. It inspires and guides us in thoughts, speech, and action. It is not always dependent on words. Instead, it comes in forms of clarifying insight, sudden inspirations, creative ideas, intuitive knowing, hunches, feelings, and spontaneous impulse. You may not actually hear the "voice," but may simply experience knowing and knowing what to do without having figured it out.

Inner guidance or direct knowing is a spiritual experience that, when received within the silent mind, becomes a source through which we receive new meaning in life, and it reveals to us our life's inherent meanings. When we experience ourselves in stillness, we intuit a way of using our mind to receive moment-to-moment guidance from the infinite universe. The spiritual teachings and principles then no longer seem foreign or irrelevant to daily life, and are no longer gleaned from books and/or teachers only. The teaching taught within will be pertinent to us.

Education and life experience provide us only partial and incomplete knowledge. Take courage to let go of what we know. Knowing we do not know will dramatically heighten our motivation to learn the new way of communication. The moment you know what you do not know, is the moment that you open yourself to true knowing, the infinite ocean of knowledge, not residing in human beings but in the vast universe.

Sadhana practice including *yoga asana*, meditation, *pranayama*, etc., is to learn and experience how to quiet the mind and to purify the body. When our body has been purified, calmed, and sensitized through *sadhana*, we become thoroughly familiar with the feeling of being-centered, at peace, and in harmony with ourselves. The impulses coming from the infinite will reverberate through us with more clarity and we will decipher the messages with greater ease.

Ancient Wisdom

Sutra 3.55: This direct knowing (*pratibha*) is comprehensive and transcendent. It is the pristine truth arising from unconditioned and undivided intelligence in the eternal present.

Direct knowing arises in the inner stillness when the mind is out of the way. Unbounded consciousness illuminates for us whatever we need to know when we need to know it. In the leap from knowledge to wisdom, we first notice an occasional flash of intuition. In the silence of meditation we begin to have more and more insight from the nameless formless. Once our inner gaze is continuously directed beyond the inane chatter of the mind and the contents of awareness, we can live immersed in the wisdom of direct knowing. We become the fullness of unbounded consciousness, free from mind/body limitations.

Practice

1. Practice the sequence: ask, listen, and action. Ask for guidance, listen inwardly for your deepest impulses, and dare to do what these prompt you to do when you have a decision to make in daily life.

2. Practice accessing your greater capacity to be aware of hearing the inner voice through your senses, impulses, feeling, and hunches, going beyond your best reasoning.

3. Practice the concept, "Know we do not know." Let go of our partial knowing and open our mind to the larger perspective and more comprehensive outlook.

4. Ask inwardly to yourself like a wave of the ocean, a cell to the brain, a grain of sand to the desert, a blade of grass, or a cloud to the sky and the answers will be revealed to you.

5. Ask the following question with absolute stillness of the mind when you are about to make a decision: "I want to do what you would have me do, what would you have me to do?"

6. Practice on easy things first, like what to buy, or what to eat, or what to wear so that when you are faced with a decision about something more important, you will be in the habit of seeking silent counsel from the universal wisdom available to you in the depths of your own consciousness. When you are in a store buying apples or other items, for example, instead of choosing the ones you would usually buy, pause inwardly for a moment and silently ask, "Should I buy red, green, or yellow today?" and then buy the ones you are prompted to buy.

Be Indifferent
A way of peaceful and truthful living

Story

In a small fishing village in Japan, there lived a young, unmarried woman who gave birth to a child. Her parents felt disgraced and demanded to know the identity of the father. She was afraid to tell the truth, the truth being that the fisherman she loved had told her, secretly, that he was going off to seek his fortune and would return to marry her. Her parents persisted. In desperation, she named Satori, a monk who lived in the hills, as the child's father.

Outraged, the parents took the child up to the temple, pounded on the door, and handed the child to Satori. The parents said, "This child is yours and you must take care of him!" "Is that so?" Satori said, taking the child in his arms, waving goodbye to the parents.

A year later, the fisherman, the real father, returned and married the woman. At once, they went to Satori to beg for the return of the child. "We must have our child," they said. "Is that so?" said Satori and handed the child to them.

Teaching

Can we remain calm when people scream in our face? Can we not raise our voices when we get mad and angry? Can we keep the same happy and serene state whenever we have to face failure or success? Can we live life like Satori, to be indifferent when facing all life situations? The world in which we live is a school, and life itself is the only real teacher who offers many opportunities for us to experience. The lessons of experience are hidden, and we are not to overreact but to respond firmly rooted in peacefulness. What we are searching for, striving to achieve, and setting goals for only brings us temporary pleasure and sorrow, high and low, satisfaction and disappointment, as in the law of opposites and duality. If everything we encounter in the world is short-lived, what is the point to react differently or lose sleep over it?

Our sorrow, fears and anger, regret and guilt, envy, plans, and cravings live only in the past or in the future. We cannot do anything to change the past, and the future will never come exactly as we plan and hope for. When we stay in the present, there is no struggle, no problem, never was, and never will be. When we release the struggle, let go of our mind, throw away our concerns, and flow and relax into the world, we then flow into being and burst into joy of an unreasonable happiness. Every time we look around at the earth, the sky, the trees, the desert, the mountains, the lakes, the streams and even people, they are nothing but the embodiment of our true Self. We are free from all the bondages of the conditioned mind. We are a part of the universe and a part of the whole. We are not different from anyone else and anything else, we are one. Why should we act differently?

The practice of peaceful living is action in inaction – fulfillment of our *dharmic* duties and responsibilities while remaining in equanimity. We may act angry, sad, gentle, rough, tough, and even concerned but we are not affected by, or not to alter, our state of contentment, happiness, indifference, and consciousness. Action without attachment is always in the present and it is an expression of body, which only can exist in the present. We receive the world of abundance when we simply give and execute without attachment to the fruit of action. Then we can do anything when we find our hearts and we no longer create ripples in our mind.

The mind, however, is like a phantom and never exists in the present. Its only power is to draw your awareness out of the present. When our mind resists life, the thoughts and emotions, and when something happens to conflict with a belief, turmoil sets up so we react to the expectation of others and our own mind. If we release the expectations that the world could fulfill us, our disappointments vanish. We would continue to do whatever is necessary to live in the everyday life. Living peacefully without reasoning, staying in the present, action in inaction, and being an impartial witness are the ultimate discipline. So act, feel, and be indifferent without a reason in the world.

Ancient Wisdom

Sutra 1.2: Yoga is the restraint of the mind to equanimity.
Sutra 1.3: Then the impartial witness abides in its own nature.

Once the mind has become purified through practice of meditation, the mind will not rush to interpret or dramatize the appearance; the customary inner chatter gives way to pure illumination of just what is. The impartial witness is the only one here to observe the outer or inner landscape. This is a very peaceful and happy state. This is yoga.

Practice

1. Watch your thoughts and emotions indifferently, like watching a movie, but don't get involved when you close your eyes during your meditation sessions.

2. Watch your thoughts or emotions when you face a life situation and observe impartially whether you react to the situation with emotion or you simply respond the situation calmly and peacefully.

3. Go to a yoga class you have never been to before or go to a controversial lecture to experience being open-hearted and indifferent.

4. Experiment getting mad or even yelling at someone or something, but beholding a grace and smile within. It is a bit extreme but great practice.

5. Ask yourself often, "What time is it? Where am I?" and always contemplate the answer "It is NOW and I am HERE."

6. Feel the flow and romance of life, such as falling in love, in-the-zone athletic performance, the flow of creative writing, doing dishes or any small acts in daily life. Experience the flow of energies that pierce deeply into your body and into the world. Then you will think about life less and feel it more and truly enjoy even the simplest things in life, no longer addicted to achievement or world entertainments.

7. Practice meditation and meditate in every action of your daily life. Watch the world as it is. You will be free from the world's turbulences.

8. Watch the ripples of your mind so you are no longer compelled to overreact every time a pebble drops.

Transcendental Sexuality: Above and Beyond
The contemplative relationship

Story

There was a perfect young monk, Bobo Roshi. He got up earlier, sat in the meditation garden longer, chopped more wood and carried more water than anyone else in a secluded Zen temple. He never climbed over the monastery walls to visit the geisha houses as the other monks did occasionally. He lived this way for fourteen years, working on his koan without break. He did everything just as it was supposed to be done, and even more. However, he still could not find the answer to this koan and his enlightenment.

Late one night after a long meditation in the garden he decided to leave the monastery. He climbed over the fences, stopped concentration on his koan, and walked aimlessly on the streets of Kyoto until he found himself in the floating world of the sensual pleasure district.

A geisha gestured to him through drawn shades. He went into her room and was served tea and saki, and was then embraced by her. Everything fell away, time ceased to exist, and space emerged into vastness as they sat face to face, held hands, danced, and made love. His sense of nothingness and unity of universe, and his search for the answer of the koan and enlightenment suddenly flashed into the state of consciousness. He wept and laughed with joy and gave the geisha his beloved rosary beads. When he went back to the monastery his *satori* (enlightenment) was confirmed by his astonished abbot.

Teaching

For some, sexuality leads to sainthood and even liberation like Bobo Roshi. For others, it is the road to hell and suffering. As most of us know, conventional religion teaches that sexuality and spirituality are somewhat mutually exclusive, if not antagonistic. There are many rationales for finding them incompatible. Saints Paul and Augustine equate desire with Original Sin. Hindus see sexuality as illusion or *maya*, and a major obstacle to liberation. The belief found in the East and West alike is that sexual abstinence and freedom from lust are essential prerequisites for enlightenment. Even in the modern culture, few of us have been taught to see sexuality as a spiritual path, and many of the qualities that make up the spiritual life can be experienced and refined through sexuality.

Transcendental sexuality is our most intimate form of communion, a mutual opening and meeting beyond words and concepts from our deepest and most vulnerable parts. Such communion is only made possible when there is openness, acceptance, and wholeness with each partner.

Transcendental sexuality is an act of surrender when we stop judging our partners, when we simply give all our hearts to our partners, and when we become more sensitive to subtleties of our sense and sensuality.

Transcendental sexuality is the union of opposites. In the Hindu Tantras, the Shakti or goddess is considered the primal energy of the world, and the male deity (often Shiva) symbolizes meditative stillness. In Buddhist Tantra, the female deity symbolizes emptiness and wisdom or stillness, while the male deity symbolizes compassion and action. In Taoism, union is expressed in the familiar yin and yang symbols. The female symbolizes dark, passive, soft, yielding energy and the earth, while the male symbolizes active, hard, light energy and the sun. The interaction between Yin and Yang constitutes the whole and creates unity and the universe. In the ancient Jewish mystical tradition of Kabbalah, the celestial 'King' and 'Queen' unite in sexual ecstasy to sustain the cosmos each day. It is seen to bring the human couple together on many levels of their being and also creates peace and love to reign more thoroughly everywhere above and beyond.

In many ways, sexuality is identical with the life force itself. It brings us together, serves as an expression of love, creates life, and fulfills our longing for unity and wholeness. There is an urge for unity from the polarity of energy. Sexual or physical union is an expression of that energetic union and offers a fleeting glimpse of wholeness and oneness. But the root of the physical union is spiritual awakening and oneness. From the spiritual point of view, we merge with the beloved in a state of ecstatic spiritual union from physical sensuality. So we can become awakened from the almost-endless, half-forgotten, life-transforming power of full-bodied, fully committed sexuality and sensuality.

Ancient Wisdom

Transcendental sexuality is an expression of the true love – motiveless tenderness of the heart, no expectation from our partners or even ourselves. The end of expectation is the end of *karma*. *Karma* is created when we have motives about our actions and expectations about the fruit of our actions. If one lives in a manner that creates no *karma*, then one is living in love through the sweetness of our own inner heart. The only way to know if this is the Truth is to test it in our experience. Is the sensuality I profess motiveless? Are my feelings, actions and expressions always tender? In this way we sharpen the blade of discrimination in knowing love from deceit. We thrust ourselves into the fire of uncompromising honesty to emerge a truly loving human being. (Hill, 2008)

Practice

1. Practice contemplative love, the secret of goalless sexuality and sensuality. Let the sensual impulse manifest itself as melting warmth and flowing into each other and transform 'physical lust' into the most considerate and tender form.

2. Explore your spontaneous feeling without any preconceived idea of what it ought to be, without any preconceived idea of your partner and the experience between you and your partner, since the sphere of contemplation is not what should be, but what it is.

3. Be a watcher of and experience the sensations that arise from sexuality and sensuality without labeling and identifying with the mind and then transcend the sensations into vastness and wholeness.

4. Practice, "Love is motiveless tenderness of heart," giving without expecting anything in return and selfless love without clinging to your partner or being possessive.

Seasonal Celebrations
Shift consciousness from Manifested to Un-manifested

Story

One day a man on a street asked Zen master Satori, "Master, will you please write for me some maxims of the highest wisdom?" Satori immediately took his brush and wrote the word "Attention." "Is that all?" asked the man. "Will you not add something more?" Satori then wrote twice running, "Attention. Attention." "Well," remarked the man rather irritably, "I really do not see much depth or subtlety in what you have just written." Then Satori wrote the same word three times running, "Attention. Attention. Attention." Half angered, the man demanded, "What does that word 'Attention' mean anyway?" And Satori answered gently, "Attention means attention."

Teaching

Paying attention may seem like a very simple thing, but we pay attention much less than we might think, because our minds are the checkerboard of crisscrossing reflection, opinions, and prejudices. We identify everything that happens in us and around us with our mind, and we do not pay attention to the thing as it is, like season changes and seasonal celebrations.

Celebrations to mark seasonal change have been practiced by most of culture since the ancient times. These celebrations acknowledge not only the outward seasonal changes but also the symbolic rhythms of our lives. In taking the time to honor these festivals and celebrate seasonal changes, we honor our own symbolic process of unfolding. In this way we cooperate with the natural life progression and life cycle and live with a true pervading consciousness.

A season is a relatively stable segment of the life cycle but it is not stationary or static. Summer has a different character from winter, spring and fall. Twilight is different from sunrise. No season is better or more important than any other. Each has its necessary place and contributes its special character to the whole. It is an organic part of the total cycle. Each season has different effects on us physically and psychologically. If we fight and resist the changes, the consequences are unpleasant ones. If we simply accept, surrender to, and embrace the ocean of changes we become a part of the changes and a part of the whole.

Everything has its own season. A time to be born or to die is the nature of its season and holds true for the course of our individual lives. The life cycle is the name given to the pattern and shape of our lives from birth to death. It is unique for each of us, but it is also universal. There is a biological dimension to this life cycle – birth, adolescence, adulthood, old age, and death. Each stage has its own transformation and spiritual challenge to be met, its own satisfactions and joys. No one stage is more crucial or valuable than another. Every moment of life is in fact part of the whole. Seasonal celebrations serve to remind us that life, like nature, has its own individual cycle. When we speak of people being in the "autumn of their years" or having a "May-December" romance, we subtly connect the nature and our lives.

Changes in the cycles of life manifest themselves in the forms of seasons, aging, death, birth, creation, and dissolution. They appear to be the reality. The essence of living is where most of us become a part of these forms and believe we are controlled and influenced by them. We are sad when the winter comes, we cry when people die, and we get depressed when we grow old. We get ourselves caught into the ephemeral world and dualistic existence. We have been conditioned as the human race collectively to believe that we are the body and we are the mind. As matter of fact we are the seasons and we are the cycle of life, all of which are subject to change. Only when we realize the un-manifested consciousness and stillness emanates through the manifested forms are we no longer swayed by the change of seasons and the change of the life cycle. We start residing in ever-peaceful living.

Ancient Wisdom

A Yogi's Life Cycle (*ashrama dharma*), from the *Vedanta Sanskrit-English Lexicon*: The meritorious way of life is particular to each of the four stages (*ashramas*) of life, following which one lives in harmony with nature and life, allowing the body, emotions and mind to develop and undergo their natural cycles in a most positive way. The four stages are as follows:

- Student (*brahmacharya*)
- Householder (*grihastha*)
- Sage (*vanaprastha*)
- Renunciate (*sannyasa*)

The first two stages are the way of going toward the world through the force of desire and ambition. The last two are moving away from the world through introspection and renunciation.

Practice

1. Practice daily rituals as a means of celebration of life during the times of transition from one activity to another such as awakening in the morning, meal times, returning home from work, and bedtimes.

2. Celebrate all festivals and holidays. Be aware of the consciousness among all the changes such as Thanksgiving, Christmas, and the New Year.

3. Pay attention to and dwell in all the pervading consciousness when the changes take place in the cycles of a day, week, month, season and year.

4. Pay attention to and dwell in the stillness when the changes take place in the cycle of life such as growing old, getting sick and dying.

5. Pay attention to and dwell in the peacefulness and fullness when the changes take place in the cycle of nature such as plants, trees, and animals.

Don't Play Ego Roles
"This, too, shall pass"

Story

According to an ancient Sufi story, there was a king who was continuously torn between happiness and discontentment. The slightest thing would cause him great upset or provoke from him an intense reaction. His happiness would quickly turn into disappointment and despair. A time came when he was tired of himself and of life. He wanted to get out of his situation. He fetched a wise man who lived in the mountains and was reputed to be an enlightened and wise man. The king said to him, "I want to be like you. Can you help me to bring peace, serenity, and wisdom into my life? I will pay any price you ask."

The wise man answered, "I may be able to help you. But the price is so great that the entire wealth of your kingdom would not be sufficient enough to pay for it. Therefore it will be a gift to you if you will honor it." The wise man returned to a holy mountain where he resided after the king gave his assurance. A few days later he returned and handed the king an ornate box. The king opened the box and found a simple gold ring inside the box with some letters inscribed on the ring. It read, 'This, too, shall pass'. "What is the meaning of this?" asked the king. The wise man said, "Wear this ring always. Whatever happens in life, before you judge it good or bad, touch the ring, and read the inscription. That way, you will always be at peace."

Teaching

'This, too, shall pass'. What is it about these simple words that makes them so powerful? It seems that these words provide some comfort in a bad life situation, while they would also diminish the enjoyment of so-called good things in life. Do not be too happy or too sad, because it will not last. 'This, too, shall pass' makes you aware of the fleetingness of every life situation. The sensation of the fleetingness is due to the transience of all forms and ego identification.

Ego, or the egoic state, is when we identify ourselves with the conditioned mind. I become "I-ness," we become "mine-ness," and we become collective "us-ness." Everything in the world becomes nothing but a projection of the ego-centered self. We start playing temporary and egoic roles at every life situation, as a listener, speaker, emotional being, stressed being, happy being, and/or joyful being. These temporary roles usually disappear after a period of time. Once we thought what we were, the role we played became nothing, but appeared to be a dream.

We play social roles and also identify ourselves as these roles in a respective society and culture. Once we thought we were students, teachers, workers, parents, politicians, leaders, and others, but when time elapses, the roles no longer exist, and we then wonder who we are now and what role we play again. We seem to get lost in the midst of role shifting. The cycle of role-playing and ego identification becomes short-lived and provides little stability in the state of being-ness.

Feeling inferior or superior, becoming defensive, upset, negative, paranoid, and even schizophrenic in defending values, beliefs, opinions, national and cultural pride, are all examples of ego identification or role-playing. They are pathological as a result of the conditioning from past experiences, knowledge, concepts, cultures, and, of course, the mind.

Ancient Wisdom

Sutra 3.3: In meditation the true nature (*svarupa*) of the object shines forth, not distorted by the mind. That is *samadhi*.

In *astanga yoga* we have been given several practices – *asana, pranayama, pratyahara*, etc., but *samadhi* is not a practice. It is a shift in identity from the ephemeral corporeal self to the conscious indweller. When "that which is looking" sees the appearance, it appears in its true nature (*svarupa*), undistorted by thought, feeling or personal history. The shift to the witnessing Self is persistent; *avidya*, ego, attachment, aversion and fear have burned away in *sadhana*.

Samadhi does not mean withdrawing from the world; it only means that we see clearly 'that which is', without distortion from the mind. Because of the inner fulfillment in the blissful state we are no longer needy of things from the world – materially, emotionally or spiritually. We are finished with the wheel of *karma* as all our actions are performed without motive. We are happy and content, just being.

Practice

1. Practice the process of resolving ego identification and role-playing with the following steps: Aware of it, Identify it, Experience it, Accept it, Surrender it, and Resolve it (AIEASR).

2. Practice Sufi's saying, "This, too, shall pass," when you encounter each life situation. You can create a space between the true Self, life events or situations, and thought, so you do not have to react to the event.

3. Practice non-resistance, non-judgment, and non-attachment to dis-identify ego and role-playing and to live in a true state of freedom and enlightenment.

4. Feel life in you and in everything, then the ego identification subsides.

5. Make peace in every moment, and now and then the ego ceases.

6. Experience oneness with life, with love, live within, and dance within.

7. Don't seek the truth, but cease to cherish opinions.

Obtaining Mystical Consciousness
A true source of energy

Story

One day I was driving on a highway on the way to San Francisco and listening to Eckhart Tolle's lecture on "Stillness in the midst of the world." I started paying close attention to the passing trees, passing cars, lights and other objects, trying to find the stillness in all without labeling and identifying with everything I encountered.

Gradually I was having the feelings of suspension, floating, slow motion, beauty, perfection, love for all, satisfaction, gratitude, being, and amid a space that exists in all directions. I became aware of my physical body as an energy body that was only part of a much larger energy field consisting of everything else in the universe. I experienced the entire universe looking out on itself through my awareness and my energy body...

Teaching

The physical world we are experiencing is made out of energy and a vast system of energy. There is nothing solid about our universe. Matter is only energy vibrating at a certain level. In the beginning, matter existed only in its simplest form, the element we call hydrogen. That is all there is in the universe, "Hydrogen."

We human beings see this manifested world as a matter of competition for energy, although we are unconscious of it, and thus have the tendency to, and strive to control and dominate others. We want to 'win' the energy between people and even between nations. We have always sought to increase our personal energy and collective energy in the manner we have learned from this conditioned mind, by seeking to psychologically steal the energy from others, and this underlies all human conflicts in the world.

It is a recent phenomenon that mystical consciousness has become recognized and publicized as a way of being that is actually attainable, and a way that has been demonstrated by the more esoteric, spiritual, yogic, and even religious practitioners. But for most of us living in the world, this consciousness only remains as an intellectual concept to be talked about and debated. However, for a growing numbers of spiritual aspirants, this consciousness becomes experientially real because we are aware of it and we experience flashes and glimpses of this state of mind during the course of our living. This experience is the key to ending human conflicts and becoming enlightened. During this experience we are receiving energy from another source, the true source of energy, no longer competing against another human being or race, and we are able to learn to tap in at will.

When we start to appreciate and be aware of the beauty and uniqueness of thing, when we fall in love with everything we encounter and people we meet without wanting something from them, and when we are in the state of being and completeness, we start receiving energy from the true source and no longer have a desire to compete with others for the energy. When we are at the level where we feel love for all in front of us, then we start sending the energy back to others and the universe.

So start connecting with energy from plants, trees, animals, people, life situations, and of course the mystical consciousness. Then we become at first excited, then euphoric, and then love, and tap into the true source of energy and sustain the state of love and consciousness, which certainly helps the world and directly helps us.

Ancient Wisdom

Hastamalakiyam: Essence of Vedanta in Twelve Verses, 8th century (from the introduction): Awakening to the Self occurs as a result of two simultaneous processes: We turn inward in meditation to embrace the sweetness of peace and bliss that is our true nature; at the same time, we release our attachments to the stuff of the world and the drama of our mental entanglements. As the mind becomes purified, luminous Self-radiance fills our being. We become the blissful Self.

Practice

1. Practice transcending human conflicts, then we begin to break free from the competition over mere human energy, and finally we are able to receive our energy from other sources such as, plants, trees, nature, consciousness, and even people.

2. Practice detecting energy flow among people and learn to tap into the flow of that energy.

3. Be aware that food is a way of gaining energy through total appreciation, taste, prayer before meals, and by making eating a holy experience.

4. Become more sensitive to energy in all things and then learn to take energy from those energy sources.

5. Open to connect to all, and feel the sensation of being filled up.

6. Allow love to enter you and flow into you, then feel unconditional love for everything, trees, people, or objects.

7. Look at a tree or plant and begin to admire its shape and presence. The appreciation grows into an emotion of love. This feeling is one we may remember love as a child for our mother, as a youth for the "puppy love," as an adult when you fall in love… Now you are in love with everything, while any particular love exists as a general background.

Homecoming

Awaken to the spiritual evolution

Story

A little boy, Shakracharaya, lived 1500 years ago in India. At age 8, he realized his life did not belong to this ephemeral world and decided to become a *sadhu*, a renounced monk. But his mother refused his persistent requests. One day while he was swimming in a river he started screaming, "Help! Help! Alligator got my legs." The whole village, including his mother, gathered along the bank of the river but no one dared to enter the river to save the little boy at a possible risk of their own lives. Shakracharaya then said to his mother, "Dear mother, the alligator promises to let go of me if you allow me to leave home and become a spiritual seeker." At the despair of losing her son, his mother agreed with the terms of condition.

Shankracharaya became a great saint and metaphysicist. He brought forth the ancient spiritual teaching *advaita vedanta* – nondualistics, oneness in all forms. He also created 10 lineages in India as a form of outer expression of the un-manifested state for people to experience the formlessness or oneness.

Teaching

Spiritual evolution is realization of an inner calling like Shankracharaya's life. For someone else it is a gradual process and may take one's entire life or several lives to realize the awakening because of our karmic predisposition. For some others it means dramatic life events served as a precursor to the awakening. Guided by our intuition, we then know precisely what to do and when to do it. Our sense of purpose becomes satisfied by the thrill of our evolution, by the elation of receiving intuition, and by watching closely as our destinies unfold. We humans start slowing down, becoming more alert and vigilant for the next meaningful encounter that comes along, we start grasping how beautiful and spiritual the natural world really is, and we start seeing trees, rivers and mountains as temples of great power to be held in reverence and awe.

Spiritual evolution is realization of presence by transcending the past and the future. Spiritual evolution as a future event and as a past event has no meaning because they represent only thought-forms or forms of accumulative knowledge or concepts. Nothing but the present moment can make us free.

When we are present, our forms – ego identifications – are dissolved, and we are no longer taken or trapped by the forms. When we weaken the forms and even lose the forms we become transparent to the light of consciousness and reveal the state of consciousness within us. So the fewer forms with which we identify, the higher state of spiritual evolution we become, regardless of when we started dissolving the form of the physical body. Practical examples of living in this awakened state are when we get old and become less 'doing' and more 'being', when we are in the state of being thought-free in a meditation session, and when outer purpose of life is in alignment with inner life purpose. Then we start a process of returning to movement, dissolving the forms, and returning to the home where we came from, nothingness, formless, and un-manifested consciousness.

We still can have work, responsibilities, relationships and even romance. But first we have to become aware of the awakening process and diligently practice detachment or even dissolution of forms. We have to stabilize our channel with the universe. We then are no longer a part of, and susceptible to, the power struggle for outer purposes of life. We enter a higher relationship with the world around us when we connect romantically – love in tenderness of heart, and we never pull away from the path of our individual evolution. Once we have up and seen the world as a mysterious place that provides everything we need, then we are ready for the evolutionary flow.

Ancient Wisdom

Living with the Himalayan Masters, by Swami Rama: We all know what to do and what not to do, but it is very difficult to learn how to be. Real knowledge is found not in knowing but rather in being.

We learn 'how to be' in the stillness of meditation; this is our essential being. When we can live from the fullness of the inner Self, we live in true wisdom.

Practice

1. Practice having and being comfortable with less – less material, less possession, less dependency on things or people, less emotion, and even less thought.

2. Practice detachment to the world of forms, including everything we experience in the world, and see these forms translucent to the light of mysterious consciousness, the formless, and the un-manifested.

3. Contemplate an inner life purpose, revealing the higher state of spiritual evolution through meditation, yoga, and/or other forms of self-realization and awakening.

4. Reconcile the inner life purpose with the outer life purpose, life forms we all experience to fulfill the dreams of others and our own conditioned minds.

5. Recognize thoughts as forms and take an observer position. When thoughts come, be aware and ask, "Why do these particular thoughts come now and how do they relate to my life situation?"

6. Being aware of the process of conscious evolution and stay alert to every coincident and every answer the universe provides for us. Taking an observer position helps us release our need to control and to attach. It places us in the flow of evolution.

7. Let our perception of beauty and iridescence lead our way to the place and people who have answers for us. Then we become more luminous and attractive.

8. When people cross our path, there is always a message for us. Whether or not we can receive the message is dependent upon our awakening state. As we become aware we should stop what we are doing at hand, no matter what, and find out the message we have for that person and that the person has for us. Our intention then slows down and becomes more purposeful and deliberate.

Playing the Edge
Gateway to the Inner Body

Story

Once I read a story from a book titled *Yoga: The Spirit and Practice of Moving into Stillness* by Erich Schiffmann, a longtime student of Krishnamurti. His story resonates with my experience and deepens my understanding of the physical form of yoga:

"One incident I remembered most clearly at the end of an Iyengar's yoga class. It had been a very intense class and difficult class. During the *shavasana*, I went particularly deep. I remembered being very quiet, very centered, and yet very wide awake. Iyengar must have noticed this because he came over to me afterward and said, 'You see, it takes Krishnamurti twenty years to get your mind quiet. I can do it in one class.' His methodology worked for me. It was not just physical, as is the common criticism of his teaching not being spiritual. This hard physical practice and presence of the body becomes the most practical, grounded and easiest way to access the spiritual being and meditative state."

Teaching

Our physical body has enormous intelligence governing the millions of tasks at once. The mind is only a part of that intelligence, otherwise the mind would ruin our physical body, not to mention our earth. But most of us are not aware of that intelligence because we have been trapped in the mind's intelligence, the mental noises. When our senses dwell in the inner universe of body, inhabit the body, and are taken away from mental identification, we are rooted in our own being, presence, and the entire energy field. We connect to the great intelligence which is much greater than the mind.

The physical body has an inner sense of aliveness and is a gateway to the presence of the inner body. So to connect to our essential being is to inhabit the body. To inhabit the body is to sense the aliveness of the body as an integral part of the whole energy field. It can happen at any time and in any form of activity as long as we start paying attention.

Yoga, as an example, is the process of awareness and embodiment wherein we attend to these subtle shifts in sensations, feeling, and even identity, the most beautiful inner music. Yoga is not about achieving elaborate *asanas* but rather growing more beautiful, strong, flexible, and connected to our source – the inner body which is even closer to our heart than our feet and hands because it is the true essence of who we are. Proceeding step by step and edge by edge, we start paying attention to what we are doing and being sensitive to the changing sensations of the body, to stretches and exertions of the subtler sensations, and we become more in-tune with our body as the gateway to our inner body.

Ancient Wisdom

Sutra 2.54: When the mind is withdrawn from sense-objects, the sense-organs also withdraw themselves from their respective objects and thus are said to imitate the mind. This is known as *pratyahara*.

The senses are slaves to the mind and go wherever the mind directs. If the mind is fascinated with the contents of awareness, the senses reach out into the appearance and bring the mind all the juice the mind has an appetite for. If the mind turns inward, becomes quiet and directs its gaze to the joyous equanimity of just breathing in and breathing out, the senses also become quiet. So we see here that *pratyahara* is the mind withdrawing from external stimulation and focusing on the inner landscape; thus the senses likewise become withdrawn.

As a practical matter we can't always sit cross-legged in the dark, breathing in the bliss, but we can remain centered in the inner quiet as we live our life. *Pratyahara* can be cultivated so that the senses are not such a distraction when we are focused on the task at hand.

Practice

1. Close your eyes, start sensing aliveness of your right foot and ask yourself, "Is there any way I know my right foot still exists?" When you feel the sensation – a shift of feeling and identity – then move to the left foot, right hand, left hand, and then entire body, a sensation of one energy body that connects to the greater energy field.

2. Feel the connectedness to the higher source from the sensation derived from inhabiting the body when you contract or lengthen the muscles, tendons, and ligaments during an activity.

3. Learn to create an energy flow that is attractive to you during your *yoga asana* practice or other forms of embodiment.

4. Enjoy working with intensity in any activity and it means more energy flow at any given moment so we can experience more sensations of happiness, sadness, openness, and connectedness.

5. When you practice *yoga asana*;
    - Look for the first edge when you come into a pose. Feel the edge, but do not rush through it. Stop moving,

deepen your breath, and be aware of the edge sensation diminishing before going deeper. Proceed slowly, edge by edge, until you reach the "maximum" edge where the muscles begin to hurt.

- Use your breath and energy flow to nudge into your edges and be watchful and patient.

- Learn to wait until your body is ready to move and listen to the inner cue to action.

- Flirt with tight spots by pressing gently, by changing the strength or character of breathing, by increasing or decreasing energy, or by doing several repetitions of the *asana*. Do not force through it.

Spiritual Self Healing
Fountain of Joy

Story

One day I had an overwhelming sadness that permeated through the evening and into the next day. I could not snap out of it even though I was totally aware of the state, and I even went on with the day and had morning *satsang* and *asana* practice and other daily chores. I noticed I was short with everyone and did not want to socialize with anyone. I sensed the sadness rising out of uncertainty of a life circumstance in which I was totally trapped. It brought out a new state of low energy and unhappiness in me. I knew that I needed to do something to connect to the higher source, to raise my energy and to start healing myself.

Then there was an urge for me to go to the ocean beach. I know I am very lucky that the beach is just a few minutes away. As I walked along the beach I started paying attention to the power, beauty, aliveness, and vastness of the ocean, water, waves, birds, sands, shells… After a while I lost track of time and I began to smell the moist freshness of the ocean, listening to the symphony of ocean waves and the sounds of birds, feeling the rising energy within, and sensing the connection to everything around me… I sat down in a grassy sand dune and took in all the beauty with the mind and every cell of the body before I closed my eyes.

I felt energy surging into my body and started feeling the sadness and the exact location of the sadness. I felt a sense of heaviness and a "rock"-like sensation at the top left of my crown. I began channeling the energy towards the "rock." It became lighter and lighter and eventually it disappeared and then I felt another rock appear over at other side of the crown. I started sending the energy there and it also dissolved after awhile. Now I felt a sense of release, lightness, happiness, and love to all that existed in me and beyond and dwelled myself into a state of trance, tranquility, and the fountain of joy...

When I opened my eyes, there was nothing left in my body and my mind but a vast beauty of ocean, waves, birds, sands, shells, music, and love inside of me...

Teaching

The true healing is to get back to the source, the all-providing source of energy; other than that is just a temporary fix. Any resistant thoughts and actions behave like barricades to block the power of energy. Unspoken fear raised from uncertainty and all mental identifications creates blocks or crimps in the body's energy flow. It then blocks, evolves, and ultimately results in anxiety, stress, disease and even death. So ideally these blocks need to be addressed before they develop into a full state of illness. We have to engage in this attitude with full awareness and alertness and adopt a positive and spiritual outlook that enables us to stay healthy.

The feeling of the fountain of joy and love reveals, as a birthright, the source of energy that never deserts us. It accompanies us regardless of our life situations, age, time and space, when we become aware of our connection to the source. It radiates to every single cell of the body and emanates through you, others, and the world around you. The joy raised from within permeates into the body, the mind, and the soul. We feel the love to all and feel the vibration heal all the mental and physical illness.

As most recent medical research indicates, more than 75 percent of all diseases are caused by our mental states. Through connecting to the higher source we become charged with a high level of energy, the loving and divine energy. It brings us into a joyful state and helps heal all illness in our physical, mental, and emotional bodies. We no longer are the passive recipients of the healing process but rather the healers of our own conditions. We no longer solely rely on traditional western medicine (doctor as expert and healer), hoping the doctors have all the answers for us. Then the health of the body, to a great degree, is determined by our mental process and mental state. This represents a paradigm shift in the healing process.

So accept the fact that you are the healer of your own. When you know it and experience it, and after you raise your energy up to a higher vibration and healing source, you offer healing energy that can channel through you to others without ego identification. The ego identification and ego mind creates disharmony and separation. Practice surrender to 'what is' and you then connect to the source in communion with a higher power. Instead of asking to be healed, ask to restore the perfect functioning that we all come from. Use affirmation to change negative, which is low energy vibration, to positive, which is higher energy vibration. Seek out and cherish silence, communion with the source, bathe yourself in the light, and remain with the inner state of gratitude for who you are, for that which resides within you.

Ancient Wisdom

Sutra 3.3: In meditation the true nature of our being shines forth, not distorted by the mind or emotions. That is *samadhi*.

In this description of *astanga yoga* we have been given several practices – *asana, pranayama, pratyahara*, etc., but *samadhi* is not a practice. It is a shift in identity from the ephemeral corporeal self to the conscious indweller. When "that which is looking" sees the appearance, it appears in its true nature undistorted by thought, feeling or personal history. The shift to the witnessing Self is persistent; the nature of the Self, which is full of joyous serenity, persists in all circumstances.

Samadhi means that we see clearly 'what is', without distortion from the mind. Because of the inner fulfillment in the blissful state we are no longer needy of things from the world – materially, emotionally or spiritually. We are happy and content, just being.

Practice
(following are the steps for the spiritual healing process)

1. Clear the mind through *pratyahara* (concentration) techniques, conscious breathing and other means to connect to the world around you like trees, plants, water, ocean, even furniture in your house, and try to raise your energy level as high as you can.

2. Begin to observe the beauty from everything around you and feel their energy and aliveness radiating to you in every single cell of the body.

3. Concentrate on a spiritual connection within and without and then feel the energy that derives from the higher source.

4. Evoke a heightened sensation of love, the fountain of joy within, and now you are ready to channel this divine energy for healing.

5. Focus energy on the block – for example, pain in the ankle, sadness, stress, headache, etc. – and use the block-like pain as a beacon to help you focus.

6. Feel the pain as much as possible and try to determine its exact location, not just the general area.

7. Now place all your attention on that specific area and be there with all of your being. You then may feel the perception of pain fading away, far into the background. The pain may become warm or tingling.

8. Then channel the divine loving energy into the exact area identified by the pain and intend the love to transform the cells there into a state of perfect functioning.

Connecting to the All-Providing Source
Song of Harmony

Story

One morning in the middle of *asana* practice, I heard vacuuming at the next door. To my surprise, instead of getting annoyed or irritated, I was listening to a beautiful chant in the midst of vacuuming. The melody of the chant was so unique I realized I had never heard it before. It synchronized with the sound of vacuuming that became an integral part of the chant. The sound of the chant brought me into the state of trance and joy… I lost track of time when the vacuum stopped suddenly and I realized the chant also stopped. My inner voice said to me, *"Please keep vacuuming so I could enjoy that chant and that state a bit longer…"*

Teaching

When we connect to the source, the all-providing source of energy, we experience beauty and love in every aspect of life, and we stay in the state of reverence, kindness, joy and tranquility. We start radiating the love to others and cause others to be empowered and experience the same state.

Spiritual Health and Healing

When we connect to the source we experience connection to everything and everyone in the universe, see the world with no separation but unification of duality – oneness – and experience the beauty of the world as it is without judgment and prejudice.

When we connect to the source and our thinking and acting are in alignment with the source we become spirited and inspired, not informed or filled with ego identification.

When we connect to the source we act selflessly, take pleasure in giving, and feel the abundance and gratitude in life.

When we connect the source we tap into the all-proving source of energy and it allows us to channel the energy to heal our illness and heal others mentally, physically, emotionally, and spiritually.

When we connect to the source we are in alignment with the source of the infinite. So there is no fear for illness or even death. Illness and death are nothing but a change of our identity in time and space.

When we connect to the source people think that we are the lucky ones in life. We harmonize with the power of the source and stay in the state of union, place our attention to 'what is', the infinite supply of the universe.

When we connect to the source we pay attention to the synchronicity of life, watch the clues and coincidences that arise in our lives, and we are ready to receive the right messages at the precise time.

When we connect to the source we find our intention to feel good and be loved. As the result of the law of attraction, the universe provides us the same feeling.

When we connect to the source we even turn the annoying vacuuming into the sound of music...

Ancient Wisdom

Sutra 2.45: *Samadhi* is attained through surrender to the Self.

Patanjali is persistent in this theme of *ishvara pranidhana* (surrender, or immersion in the Self). In the sutras we see that this is the direct path to the highest state of yoga. What does this mean, exactly, to surrender? What do we do, and what state is this? Simply stated, it means for the ego to get out of the way of the silent witness – the conscious indweller. When we look out on the world it is the Self that is seeing and knowing. The ego, with its neediness and fear, has subsided. This is the state of *samadhi*, the culmination of the eight limbs of yoga.

As a practical matter, how do we live in the world in *samadhi*, without the ego? We know we are surrendered to the Self when our predominant presence is inwardly quiet, and our actions are performed without burden or drama. This is not hard; it's just that we are not accustomed to being this way because of our social conditioning. After all, this really is our true nature. The practice of *ishvara pranidhana* simply awakens us and reconditions us to remember who we are. See for yourself; after a period of practice, don't you seem to remember this state as familiar? Be patient with yourself. If you persist in this practice as a discipline, *samadhi* will arise in its fullness.

Practice

1. Practice silent meditation, *asana*, and *pranayama* to let go of all the noise in the mind and experience the love and joy that emanate from the source.

2. Practice all four paths of yoga to connect to the source: *karma yoga*, the yoga of action; *raja yoga*, the yoga of the systematic; *bakti yoga*, the yoga of devotion; and *jnana yoga*, the yoga of wisdom and discrimination.

3. Align with universal synchronicity, pay attention to the clues and coincidence, and be ready to receive the messages from the source.

4. Remain in the inner state of gratitude and be thankful of what is.

5. Renounce ego driven energy and harmonize with the all-providing source of energy.

6. Raise the energy as high as you can by connecting to the world around you like trees, plants, water, ocean, and even furniture in your house.

Breaking Free from Samskara, the "Pain Body"
Tense presence of light

Story

"Why did not you call me?" "Why did you treat me like this?" "You should have written to me." "You must have changed." "Why did you not understand me?" "You caused my misery, upset, and sadness." … The consequence of my story is not hard to predict, is it? Fight, break up, resentment, sadness, unhappiness, stress, anxiety, low energy, loss of life purpose, and even disease to list only a few.

Teaching

Does this sound familiar when we deal with relationships with others, especially loved ones? We blame others for our own misery. "It is all your fault," the noise of the mind says to us.

Most of us are not aware of our own "pain body" – *samskara*, or the life debt. We do not even realize that we always repeat the same story with the same person or even with different persons at different times? We repeat the same life story because of our life, or even past lives' debt – *samskara*.

Samskara is triggered by the unconscious mind stuff, jealousy, lust, envy, egoism, anger, greed and hatred. It is unconscious to us only when we totally identify ourselves with our conditioned mind and emotion and when we are trapped in egoic self.

We all have debts or *samskara* in our lives that cause us to suffer and experience difficulties in life. Only through experience and awareness of consciousness do we start paying back the debts accumulated in the past. Only through the power of presence, the presence of light, and the state of consciousness brought forth does *samskara* become transcendental and transparent, where it no longer expresses itself. Only when we dwell on *sat-chit-ananda*, existence, knowledge, and bliss absolute, when we start understanding heart, equal vision, balanced mind, faith, devotion, and wisdom, when we gain inner spiritual strength to resist temptation and to control the mind, and when we free ourselves from the unconscious acts, only then do we truly experience neither suffering nor creation of new *samskara*. We finally break free from the *samskara* and the cycle of incarnation.

Ancient Wisdom

Sutra 1.19: Even awakened ones who have some mastery over mutable nature return to take another body because of *samskaras*.

As we continue our practice of meditation, our mastery increases over more and more subtle objects of contemplation. We build the momentum of inner stillness and absorption in our formless inner Self. Through this momentum the *samskaras* lose potency and ultimately dissipate, never to return. If we leave the body before this final attainment, subtle attachments call us back to the objects of our interest. Once thoughts in the mind and *samskaras* no longer arise, we are finished, we have attained liberation from the wheel of *karma* to merge into the bliss of universal consciousness. If this state is attained while still in the body, we may not notice when the body falls away.

Practice

1. Be aware of, and be intensely present when the pain body, *samskara*, starts expressing itself. The body pain cannot express itself with presence of light – the conscious state.

2. Experience the pain body, *samskara*, fully without reaction, judgment, or prejudice.

3. Point out unconscious triggers for your partner or your spiritual friends that may cause emotions and bad reactions to the pain body, *samskara*.

4. Practice divine virtues like selfless love, surrender, non-attachment, oneness and discrimination to counter the unconscious acts such as egoism, greed, anger, hatred, etc.

5. Connect to the all-providing source of energy and then *samskara* will subside.

Lose Yourself Before You Find Your Self
To perceive, not to label

Story

A Zen master and a disciple walked quietly along a mountain trail. After a long walk they sat down at an ancient pine tree and ate their simple meal of rice and vegetables. The disciple finally broke silence and asked, "Master, what is the key to Zen?" (The *nirvana* in Buddhism, *samadhi* in Hinduism, or heaven in Christianity.) The master kept silence for at least a few minutes while the disciple anxiously waited for the answer. Right before the disciple was ready to request the answer again the master said to him, "Do you hear the mountain stream?" The disciple replied, "No!" and started paying attention to the surroundings. His noisy mind began to subside and to give away to the heightened state of consciousness. "Master! Master! I heard a sound of mountain stream from far in the distance," responded the disciple at last. The master raised his finger pointing toward the stream and said, "Enter the Zen from there!" Coupled with the stillness of mind, the disciple discovered aliveness of the surroundings, where he felt he was experiencing everything for the first time, the beauty of mountain views, smell of the forest, melody of birds and water streams, and cushioned floor of the rocky mountain trail...

Teaching

'Lose yourself' means disassociating with mind identification. The mind no longer identifies who we are based on past experience, future prediction, other people's expectations, social norms, societal value, or even religious beliefs. The purpose of the mind is to serve us as an instrument to perceive the world as it is but not to comment, compare, or judge. When we think and label ourselves, others and the world around us, we become trapped in the world of duality in which we are subject to change and suffer.

When you lose yourself – the ego self – the noisy mind subsides. The higher Self reveals itself in the state of luminous space and eternity where forms, names and duality cease to exist. In this heightened and alert state, when consciousness is not absorbed in thinking or labeling, we connect to the all-providing source, the source of energy, we feel the sense of calmness and stillness in the background of the universe, we become the source of selfless love and radiate the love to others, we are unified with everyone and everything, we remain formless and un-manifested, we experience a glimpse of consciousness, *satori*, *samadhi*, or *nirvana* like the young disciple in the story.

Ancient Wisdom

Sutra 2.25: Liberation is the disassociation of the seer and the seen that brings the disappearance of ignorance (*avidya*).

The Seer is not inherently bound to objects of awareness; it only seems that way because of conditioning of the immature psyche. In the practice of meditation we are able to restrain the *thoughts in the mind*, awaken to the inner stillness, and discriminate the silent Self from the chaos of vagrant prattle. Once we know the stillness and know we are the Self, we can detach our identity from contents of awareness. Ignorance fades and wisdom emerges. This brings the end of association of *the mind* with *the conscious witness*; this is liberation.

Practice

1. Look at an object close to you, like a chair, a cup, or a glass with a great interest and curiosity. Avoid the object with words that may easily lead you to the process of thinking and mind identifying. Disassociate yourself with the history of the object, where you bought it or who gave it to you. Enjoy the perception of the object, without the noise of the mind commenting and comparing, for a few minutes then gaze slowly at everything around you.

2. Listen to any kind of sound with full awareness, attention and perception and make sure not to interpret, comment, or judge as good or bad.

3. Practice daily *yoga asana*, *pranayama*, and meditation to experience the sense of losing the egoic self and to elevate yourself to the level of a floating sensation – the higher Self.

4. Immerse yourself in reading, music, exercise, driving, and even walking so you will lose yourself and connect to the higher Self.

5. Practice energy connecting techniques like gazing at a plant, tree, river, rock, etc., without thinking or labeling.

Reveal the Love Within
Complete Ourselves

Story

Every day during lunchtime, a construction worker pulled out his lunch box and complained about his lunch, "Not again, peanut butter and jelly sandwich." He continued to express his disappointment of the same old peanut butter and jelly sandwich for a long period of time. Finally his co-worker got frustrated and asked him, "Why do you not let your good ol' lady fix you something else?" He then replied with a surprise, "What do you mean, my good ol' lady? I fix my own lunch every day."

Teaching

We complain about life, misery, misfortune, sadness, loneliness, unfairness, and even the peanut butter sandwich. We create our own life situations and sometimes we are even aware of them just like the construction worker in the story. We also tend to repeat the same life situation and life story over and over and wonder why…

We experience this when we identify ourselves with our mind, our thoughts, and our dramas in life. We then become those thoughts, emotions, and become entangled with unfolding dramas without consciously being aware of it. We go on with our life and think it is normal to be in the drama and to be in the state of misery because that is who we are, and plus, everyone else seems to be riding in the same boat. "Life will get better" is the optimists' belief, and "Life is going to be nothing but suffering" is from the pessimists' viewpoint. They both experience the same letdowns over a period of time. Why is that? The external world with which we identify ourselves is ever-changing, ephemeral, and unstable. Any structures and forms/names are temporary and only exist in the eyes of our minds.

We in the modern human race try to stop suffering through different means of suppressing the symptoms. Drug therapy uses chemicals to alter the state of consciousness. Psychotherapy uses our mind to settle the mind stuff. They both try to change who we are through external forces and seem to fail us every time.

There is not much choice left for us to end the suffering. To reveal the loving Self within and to complete our own Self are the seemly logical answers. They can be achieved through quieting the mind, connecting to the higher source, and seeing beauty and love in oneself, in everything and in everyone. We then complete ourselves as who we are truly. We no longer need other people's energy to fulfill our birth vision or personal legend. We no longer need materials to satisfy our soul. We no longer need other people to complete our dreams…

Ancient Wisdom

Hastamalakiyam: Essence of Vedanta in Twelve Verses (from the preface): Awakening to the Self occurs as a result of two simultaneous processes: We turn inward in meditation to embrace the sweetness of peace and bliss that is our true nature; at the same time, we release our attachments and aversions to the stuff of the world and transcend the drama of our mental entanglements. As the mind becomes purified, luminous Self-radiance fills our being. We become the blissful Self.

Living continuously in the fullness of the Self, we never again experience being insecure, needy or fearful. Being contented and serene brings contentment and serenity to others. Expressing the spontaneous joy of 'just being' brings only love from all we touch.

Practice

1. Cultivate self-love, recognize you're a divine being, and believe in love as your second nature.

2. Cultivate and reveal love within by sending loving thoughts, loving acts, and loving speech to others in need.

3. Learn to impartially watch the dramas and suffering and experience them fully without mental commentary.

4. Practice methods of quieting the mind through the systematic *raja yoga*, an eight-step approach written by Patanjali.

5. Practice mental discriminatory ability regarding the true and the relative truth.

Law of Attraction
The field of Intention

Story

In the movie *What the Bleep Do We Know*, a Japanese scientist completed an experiment regarding how human thoughts influenced the molecular patterns of water. He found that the water collected in a dam showed a simple molecular pattern, whereas the water blessed by a Zen master showed an elaborate, symmetrical pattern. Even the water collected from the same dam showed the elaborate, symmetrical pattern when the words 'Chi of Love' were placed on the bottle of water.

Teaching

Think about how our thoughts can influence the molecular patterns of water and imagine how the thoughts could affect our lives and the ways of living. One of the ancient Indian saints, Sivananda once said, "As you think, so you become." We live in a world, mostly of time, bombarded by the dramas and nuances, or consumed by the sense of pleasures. The nuances and sense of pleasures lead us to the peaks and the valleys or roller coaster rides of our emotions. Most of us believe there is nothing we can do about it. It is just a part of life, a part of our culture, a part of who I am, a part of other people's faults, a part of the human race… Through the conditioning of our mind, and living in the familiar paradigm, we have come to believe that we have little control over our life situations.

The field of intention, sometimes referred to as the field of prayer, shows us the power of our thoughts. It empowers our ability to see the ups and downs of our lives as the means to an end. It teaches us how to live our lives in a grateful abundance. When we wake up in the morning, we feel the gratitude of being alive and being offered an opportunity to experience the world of abundance, and we set a positive intention to live this very day and this very moment to the fullest with nothing but love and joyfulness. As we enter the day of broad new experiences, be aware of the state of stillness and gratitude that accompanies us in the midst of 'the world of dramas'. At the end of the day we surrender to the experiences we encountered, either good or bad, and now we are at peace with ourselves and the world around us.

The field of intention can also apply to the life of the future and the lives of others. We have the images of successful business, loving companionship, loving family, ultimate career, positive person, and living peacefully and joyfully. Send messages of positivity, healing, prayer, and love to those we love and those in need. The intentions we set and the seeds we plant will blossom and manifest themselves like a boomerang and the world will conspire to help us to realize our intentions. At this very moment of our lives we no longer suffer, no longer identify dramas as forms of suffering, and we experience the flow of life and the taste of avatar...

Ancient Wisdom

Sutra 2.36: When the yogi is firmly established in truth (*satya*), the power of fruitful action is acquired.

One grounded in truthfulness gains willpower and potency of thought and speech. Not only what one says is true, but what one says becomes true. It becomes so through no action. Even though willful, *satya* transcends *karma*. Thus is the power of intention.

Practice

1. Be aware of every thought that arrives in you and every drama that drives you, and practice the non-cooperation technique.

2. Have a small notebook handy and start watching the negative thoughts come to your mind, and record them every time they arise. Reflect on them at the end of the day.

3. Practice using the field of intention techniques in your daily life, starting small; for example, having the image of a parking lot in front of your work before you drive to work, sending a loving thought to a difficult person at work, sending healing energy to the person in need, having the image of a friend you have not seen for a long time, then see and observe what happens.

4. Use affirmation everyday to set the intention for the day, for the work, for the human interaction, etc. For example, "I am full of love," "I am positive," "I am full of energy," etc.

Universal Space Within and Without
Transcend the mind and body

Story

One day, in San Francisco at the Sivananda Yoga Vedanta Center, after I conducted a yoga class, Susan, one of the students came to ask me, "Vedantin, I have a question to ask you and I do not know how to make sense out of this." "What is it?" I responded. She said, "During the last part of relaxation and meditation my mind and body were so quiet that I felt I was transparent like an empty space. Everything else around me, the walls and the building became transparent, too. I felt that I could walk through the wall and the building because my body was connected to everything else I sensed." I told her that her experience was extraordinary and she had actually connected to the all-providing source of energy. She should try to remember that experience and the state and try to bring herself into that state very often to remind herself the world itself is nothing but the empty space...

Teaching

When we are in the meditative state we create a space around us. That space gives us a cushion to watch the world as it is. We do not have to react to the life dramas. Instead we respond to all life situations with thought-after solutions or intuitive insights. That space becomes a buffer zone in which the reaction to life situations no longer exists. We then enter the world as a true watcher and an impartial witness without judgment and prejudice, and connect to the space of the universal consciousness with ease and limitless powers just like Susan did.

The vastness of universal space, from galaxy to galaxy, is formless and nameless beyond today's science and our minds' comprehension. In everyday life we simply are a small yet integral part of the whole universe. We are the local addresses of the whole universe. We are the body, mind, and emotion as a form to experience the consciousness of universal space. If we are conscious of our existence we can sense the space between objects, subjects, life forms and even between our breath, the words, actions, thoughts, and emotions. When we can see, sense, and experience the space, we are not isolated and separated beings but human forms connected with the universal consciousness. We then start embracing the evolution of our spirituality personally and collectively as the human race and find the inner meaning and the flow of everyday life.

Connecting to the space of the universal consciousness reminds us to be conscious in ourselves, not just in everything we do, see, think, speak and act, but also conscious about the perception and readiness to receive and connect to the vastness of the universal space. We then become aware of the thoughts in the mind, sensations of bodily experience, and outbursts of emotion and start the process of transcending our mind, body and emotion.

Ancient Wisdom

Hastamalakiyam: Essence of Vedanta in Twelve Verses: When not associated with the limiting adjuncts (in the form of the body, mind and sense-organs), I (the Self) am like space.

Akasa: The example of space (*akasa*) given by Hastamalaka is in line with the traditional teaching, where *akasa* is often used in the process of revealing the *atma*. This is because *akasa* (space) has several characteristics similar to those of the *atma*, like all-pervasiveness, support of everything, free from modification, etc.

This is why meditation on space is recommended for the *vedantic* seeker as a means to familiarize with the nature of the Self (*atma svarupam*).

[Notes taken from lectures by Swami Paranarthananda, teaching in Chennai, India]

Practice

1. Meditate on space. Imagine a space like the form of a rainbow around your body, feel the space connected to the vastness of universal consciousness and your body, sense the unity of all life forms beyond your body, experience the formlessness of transparency, and dwell yourself into the state of oneness.

2. Carry that space with you when you enter the world of dramas and use that space as a cushion to delay any bodily and emotional reaction to life situations and respond to them with the intuitions of universal consciousness.

3. Recognize you are not the mind you think, you are not the body you experience, and you are not the emotion you express, you are the flow of universal consciousness.

4. Recognize 99 percent of our human body is made out of space and our body is transparent in nature even though we think we are a solid and permanent human body. Feel the connection and experience the same space we share between our bodies and the universe.

The Law of Action and Reaction
There is no such thing as an accident

Story

I'd like to share some of my correspondence for this week's Yoga Theory and Practice. The names of the correspondents have been eliminated or altered and some of the text has been edited without changing its essence.

"... I love and respect my culture; however, living here (in Japan) sometimes makes it hard... The way people think here is just different from the way I think... I believe this time God gives me what I need to grow by overcoming this matter I am facing. It is not easy and makes my inner soul painful... but I have to do it here on my own. We human beings need humans, but also we get hurt by humans as well..."

"... This past month has been the lowest time of my life. I have told my family and my doctor I am just not sure I want to stay here in this world. There is too much pain, too much on my shoulders, and I am so tired. I just want it to stop. I cannot separate from my emotions, I cry all the time. I am without hope. I try to meditate. The one nostril breathing sometimes helps me for a bit, so I do that a lot. I even do my beginning yoga CD at home. I am taking my prescriptions and going to group meetings, but it's not helping and I am tired. Just so tired..."

Teaching

Why is life full of suffering and full of colors and surprises? Do we have the choice to live one type of life rather than others? If we do, how do we do it?

We experience suffering and joy, love and hate, and likes and dislikes when we get trapped right in the center of dramas in our lives. It seems all of those human sufferings are an integral part of our lives. This is not true because our state of mind has been conditioned since we were born, and even traces back to our past lives and the collective human conditions we experience as a nation and the universe.

We have to realize that to change the paradigm we have been living for thousands of years is not an easy task. Instead of trying to change it, in our spiritual *sadhana* practice we allow things to flow into our lives at their own pace and in their own forms. We accept things as they are rather than fight against the grain or the flow. We need to be in touch with the mission of our own birth vision, which is no different from the universal spiritual evolution, to awaken the spiritual self and to connect to the all-providing source of living and let go of our egoic states... When we are in alignment with the inner purpose of life we become a cloud in the sky, a snow falling onto the ground, water flowing into the ocean... they are all going to the same place and the same source.

We are all different in the forms and names that associate and identify who we are. We experience different life situations in the way life has been put out for us. For most of time we have no choice but to surrender to the polarity of the life force. We have to live in the place in which we do not like to live, we have to work with someone that we do not care about, we have to do the things we have no interest in doing. So why do we have to do all of this? We have no choice in the form of debts (*karma*) we have accrued over the past and past lives. The only way out is to experience them and exhaust them without further attachment to the consequences of our actions, thoughts, and deeds. Then we become free and free from all the dramas in life and sufferings even as we are still in the midst of the world.

Karma signifies not only action or deed whether physical or mental but also the result of the action. The consequence is not really a separate property, but a part of the action. There is a cause, and the effect must be produced. The tree produces seeds and becomes the cause for the seeds. The cause is found in the effect and the effect is found in the cause. This is the universal chain of cause-and-effect which has no end or beginning. There is no such thing as a blind chance or accident.

Everything in nature obeys this law of cause-and-effect. Who we are, what we do, the breakout of a war, occurrence of an earthquake, diseases in the body, lightning, floods, fortunes, misfortunes, all have definite causes behind them even when our limited mind is unable to find the causes of events. Who we are and what we do in our lives today, referred to as *karma*, is the sum total of our acts, both in present life and in preceding ones. It is our own *karma* that brings us rewards and/or punishment. No one is to be blamed.

Karma is threefold. The accumulated karmas have been accrued for us from the past. It is seen in one's character, tendencies, aptitude, capacities, inclinations and desires. The fructifying karma is that portion of the past karma responsible for the present body. It is ripe for reaping. It cannot be changed nor avoided. It can only be exhausted through experience. We pay our past debts. The current karma is that karma which is now being made for the future.

In *vedantic* literature, there is a beautiful analogy explaining the *threefold karma*. The archer has already released an arrow. The arrow has left his or her hands. He or she cannot recall it. He or she is about to shoot another arrow. The bundle of arrows in the quiver on his or her back is the accumulated work. The arrow that has been shot is the fruit of the past work. The arrow about to shoot is current work.

Every action, every speech, and even every thought in the mind create karma, the action and reaction. So we can either create good karma or bad karma for us to reap later on in life or in future lives by consciously being aware of our action, speech, and thought. Going one step further, if we do not want to create karma anymore while exhausting all accumulated and fructifying karma, then we must be here and now without being attached to the fruit of action, deed, speech, or thought.

Ancient Wisdom

Yoga Vasistha (from the introduction by Swami Suryaprakash Saraswati): The first story in the *Vairagya Prakarana* does not begin with Sage Vashishtha speaking to Sri Rama, but with a very humble and modest Brahmin named Sutikshna who has gone to his guru, Sage Agastya, for spiritual guidance. When Agastya, knowing his disciple very well, asked him the cause of his confusion and grief, Sutikshna said, "Tell me, is it the performance of one's duty that will lead one to liberation, to *nirvana*, to *moksha*, or is it the renunciation of everything, going to the Himalayas and forgetting everybody and everything?"

Sage Agastya replied, "Just as a bird flies on two wings, in the same way the aspirant flies up to the goal of self-realization, to liberation, on the two wings of *karma* and *wisdom*. So it is neither one nor the other but the blending of the two. That is the art which one has to learn to evolve in spiritual life."

Practice

1. Practice acceptance to whatever comes to us in life whether considered good or bad by our conditioned minds.
2. Experience sensations and bodily expressions of suffering or happiness without being attached to these sensations.

3. Pay full attention to the tasks at hand without being attached to the consequences of the actions, either good or bad, as the fruits we reap or debts we pay from the past. We then exhaust the karmas and create no more karma for the future.

4. Constantly connect to the inner purpose of life in the midst of worldly living and then we allow the flowing peace and beauty into our lives.

Pursuing Happiness

Breaking the continuity between the past and the future

Story

Once, I fell in love. We had a deep connection at all levels, spiritually, energetically, emotionally, physically, and even at a subtle psychic level. Our lives filled with joy and love happened not just within, but also radiated outwards toward others and the world around us. We embraced and cherished each other as who we are and what we do. We shared our dreams and sorrows without commentary. We were in the flow of life and felt we were in the process of completing our life journey and our birth vision incarnated into this very life. The world was the perfect place to be and live in.

As time went on, I started developing attachments and expectations for the relationship, like we always do in our everyday lives. I wanted more time together, wanted more love to be returned, and wanted more life together. I had expectations and sometimes demanded for everything to be done with the 'reason of love'. It all sounded very logical in the mind, except the relationship began deteriorating and I started experiencing pain, sorrow, sadness, distance, isolation, loneliness, blame, and even anger sometimes at myself and others when the expectations no longer were fulfilled… I was in the middle of world drama again.

Teaching

Any demand and expectation other than 'what is' brings dissatisfaction and unhappiness, bad weather, poor air quality, too small of a house, not enough money, too fat, too thin, too big of a nose, boring job, demanding boss, energy-taxing partner, busy life, and purposeless life. We simply allow these life situations or life stories to run over and dictate our lives. We become part of the drama and the stories, are trapped into the forms, and experience the world of duality phenomenon, high and low, like and dislike, happy and sad, rich and poor, abundance and lack...

Happiness is who we are, our birthright and our birth vision. It resides within all of us. There, however, is no eternal happiness in pursuing outer purpose of life, but temporary satisfaction trying to fulfill expectations of others and ourselves. The true happiness does not derive from behaviors of others, does not come from the expectations of society, the world and ourselves, and is not from the fruits of actions we take...

So what is happiness? We can practice the elimination game called *'neti neti'*, not this not that. It is not darkness inside the heart, it is not jealousy, it is not hatred, it is not blame, it is not the house we own or the job we do, the person we possess, it is not expectation and demand other than for this moment to shape 'what is', and it is not external world where dramas and stories of life unfold...

Bring inner alignment with 'what is'. Say "Yes" to and allow the form that the moment shapes, as it is. To accept what is at this moment of life, not the stories of life, is to free us from the life stories and to break the continuity between the past and the future. Then the happiness derives from rising intelligence, far greater than the accumulated knowledge we have as conditioned. We begin smiling from within when we hear a bird chirping or see an ant crawling on our skin. We start embracing the aliveness of everything around us. Our hearts then are filled with an abundance of gratitude and selfless love.

Ancient Wisdom

Brihadaranyaka Upanishad (context by Swami Anatananda): Two thousand five hundred years ago, a story was recorded in the *Brihadaranyaka Upanishad*. The sage Yajnavalkya, who was about to leave home to wander the forest for the last part of his life, offered each of his wives their share of his property. The younger wife, Maitreyi, declined her share of his wealth, requesting, "Tell me instead, sir, all that you know."

This pleased the sage immensely and he taught Maitreyi about the great Self. At the end of his discourse, he said, "By what means can one perceive him by means of whom one perceives this whole world?" The sage's answer to his own question contains the phrase that became the classic *vedanta* practice for de-superimposition. Yajnavalkya said, "About this Self, one can only say, 'Neti neti,' not this not this. The Self is not this."

Neti neti is a *sadhana* practice of noticing our sensory perceptions, thoughts, feelings, and inner enemies, and of reminding ourselves that we are not them. We are the awareness of them. In *neti neti* we are undoing the superimposition of our small self onto our great Self.

Practice

1. Take a walk on the beach or in a forest to connect to divine energy, the true source of happiness.

2. Experience the pain and suffering fully, be present with the experience, and observe the happiness arising from the experience.

3. Bring out the smile from within yourself and in others every moment when you experience the aliveness and beauty of the smallest things around you.

4. Align forms with life situations as each moment shapes them.

5. Expectations Stone – every time you experience something other than your expectation, switch the stone from one pocket to another. It breaks the continuity between past and future.

Illusory Self
Suffering is when we hold onto the layers of ourselves

Story

The spiritual teacher, Eckhart Tolle, once told a story: He was walking along a mountain trail with a group of his students. They were watching the beauty of the mountain, streams, trees and forest; they were listening to the sound of the bird, wind, stream and forest; and they were enjoying the serenity and eternity of the universal creation… then they stumbled into a building with a big warning sign in the front that read: 'Caution! Do Not Enter. Structure not Stable.'

Teaching

Any structure is unstable and subject to crumbling. Every structure, even streams, trees, forests and mountains, will collapse and dissolve. A beautiful castle or a piece of furniture seems to last forever and have permanent nature. But they are changing in their structure right at this moment and will crumble in a very near future, especially when we compare it with the creation of the universe that lasts millions of years. It dissolves in a second.

Every living being, animal, tree, plant, and even humans are like a structure subject to change and the cycle of creation. They all will diminish and dissolve in the sense of form identified by our human conditioned mind. Every story of our life is subject to fail, every part or layer of our self will diminish. No longer a mom, no longer a teacher, no longer in charge, no longer dominate, no longer an egoic self, even no longer suffering…When we realize the truth of impermanence as the nature of our existence in the ephemeral world, the light, or the wisdom of living, shines through the layers of our mind identification.

To lose identity of who we are in the ephemeral world, we start peeling away our conditioned layers, angry self, happy self, superior self, inferior self, dominant self, and egoic self. When we lose the layers of egoic self, we suffer. We experience let-downs, sadness, unhappiness, grief, guilt, anger, resentment, doubt, and discontentment because we lost the "identity" – the form of the world we value and identify with. Most of the time, we lose sight of the fact that every form is temporary, subject to change. Sooner or later it crumbles.

The structures – stories of life, egoic self, and forms – are transparent. What lies formless is the life within. Every form we experience is a portal, gateway, or doorstep to the eternal existence only when:

>We are aware of its impermanency;

>We follow the flow of life;

>We align ourselves with the inner purpose of life;

>We connect the all-providing universal energy;

>We access the divine healing energy;

>We love all creations of the universe; and

>We experience the stillness in all forms of life.

Ancient Wisdom

Panchadasi, a 14th century *advaita* classic by Swami Vidyaranya on the metaphysics of *vedanta* and the methods that lead to the realization of the Supreme Truth ("The Stages of Enlightenment" excerpt): The conviction that there is a desirer and there is a desire for objects should be melted down in the greater conviction that the Self is the all. Thus, the pains caused by unfulfilled desires cease, like the flames of a lamp without oil. Similarly, a knower of Reality does not seek enjoyment even in objects apparently pleasing. He is convinced of their absence in the form in which they appear, their impermanence and insubstantiality, and gives up attachment to them. One cannot expect peace of mind through possession of wealth. True seekers of liberation are satisfied even with obtaining the minimum needs of life and do not ask for large possessions, for desire is never extinguished by the fulfillment of it.

Practice

1. Recognize the impermanent nature of all existence in and around you.

2. Watch and experience the changes in all forms of existence in and around you.

3. Impartially witness the emotions that arise from the changing roles in life or the peeling layers of the self.

4. Resonate with the stillness, eternity, and our life within, and with all forms of existence in and around you.

5. Follow the flow of life, the flow of inner calling, the flow of universal energy, and the flow of selfness love – love to all creations in and around you.

Portal of Enlightenment
Stop compulsive thinking

Story

In the book *Power of Now*, Eckhart Tolle told a story: A beggar asked a stranger for spare change. The stranger said, "Sorry! I have nothing to offer you. What is in the box you are sitting on?" "Nothing! Just an empty box. I have the box as long as I remember and never open it," replied the beggar. Intrigued by the answer, the stranger insisted that the beggar open the box. The beggar managed to ply the box open and to his surprise he found a box of gold…

Teaching

Does it sound familiar that we as human beings seek pleasure, satisfaction, and happiness from external sources and compulsive thinking? The concept of 'spare change' manifests in our real life in the forms of dependency, approval, attachment, lust, and blame. It becomes a source of our daily stress, anxiety, disappointment, suffering, and even diseases. We do not realize the true 'Gold' residing within each one of us.

'I think, therefore I am.' Compulsive thinking creates names, forms, labels, words, judgments, likes, dislikes, and the law of duality. It falsifies the true identity as "who we are" and casts a shadow of our own suffering. The unstoppable amount of noise in the mind increases fragmentation between the internal and external world and prevents us from accessing the garden of inner stillness, oneness inseparable from being, and unconditional happiness and joy.

The thinking mind does not grasp the light of consciousness and oneness, which only reveals its true nature when the mind is quiet and still. It is accessible to all of us. While it can be felt through awareness, it is not understood mentally. Nature is the state of feeling oneness with all beings, being one with the manifested world around us – such as mountains, streams, animals, and even fellow human beings – as well as being one with the un-manifested Self within. That is the end of suffering, the enlightenment, as Buddha said.

Enlightenment is not super accomplishment, wealth, accumulated materials, or intellect. It is like an infinite vastness of being and is ever-present in one's life, beyond the myriad of life forms that are subject to birth and death. It is the state of wholeness and is, therefore, at peace. One may see a glimpse of the truth, enlightenment, not only beyond the manifested world of forms and names, but also deep within the forms and names.

Ancient Wisdom

Yoga Vasistha, VI.1:82: Rama asked, "If even such a great *siddha-yogini* as Chudala could not bring about the spiritual awakening and the enlightenment of King Shikhidhvaja, how does one attain enlightenment at all?" Vasistha said, "The instruction of a disciple by a preceptor is but a tradition; the cause of enlightenment is but the purity of the disciple's consciousness."

Practice

1. The very first stage of practice is to recognize the compulsive thinking mind, then use the following modalities as portals to access a glimpse of enlightenment:

2. Focus on one thing at a time and try to be single-minded.

3. Feel oneness or connection with everything around you, tree, grass, dirt, even fellow humans.

4. Feel oneness or space within you.

5. Be aware of the sensations of breath, body, and the subtle energy flow within.

6. If you have time, meditate, breathe consciously, and do yoga.

Mystical Reunion
Whoever brought me here will have to take me home

Story

The great Sufi mystical teacher, Rumi, once told a story: A tavern has many wines with delightful colors, forms and tastes, a place where human beings enter with an entrancing variety of desires and wants. Fermentation, like the ancient alchemist transmitting base metal to gold and human suffering to consciousness, is one of the oldest systems for human transformation. When grapes combine with their juice and are closed up together for a period of time in a dark place, it results in spectaculars. That is why they do not know who is who when two drunks meet. After some points in the tavern, longing for the source prevails. The drunk sets off from the tavern and starts the return; as the Quran says, "We are all returning."

It was 4 a.m. A drunk left a tavern and walked through a town aimlessly. A police officer stopped him and asked, "Why are you out wandering in the street in the middle of night?" "Sir," replied the drunk, "if I knew the answer to that question, I would have been home hours ago."

Teaching

We human beings set off amidst the world from the source and immediately start searching for the route back to where we came from. We learn and conform to the values and expectations of others. We form our own identities. We get caught and trapped in everyday dramas. We try to pursue happiness, a hopeful journey taking us back to our home.

Where is home and the source? How do we get there? The answer obviously is not to chase one dream after another, because they only provide short-lived and temporary satisfaction. We often thought we found the key to the kingdom, but a day, a week, or a month later, we feel empty handed and get lost in the street in the middle of the night again.

Mystical experiences from within and without in everyday life reveal the subtle shift of identify from stern to ecstatic and from everyday life to esoteric. We start immersing and exploring the mystery of union with the divine and honor the variety and simultaneity of mystical reunion. The experiences give us a sense of feeling, as a meadow feels when it hears thunder, as tired eyes look forward to sleep, as joy for the spirit, and as health for the body. Then we are at home all the time and do not have to search for the route back to the source.

Ancient Wisdom

Yoga Vasistha, II:33 (Vasistha teaches Rama about the mystical state): When the mind is at peace and the heart leaps to the supreme truth, when all the disturbing thought-waves in the mind-stuff have subsided and there is an unbroken flow of peace and the heart is filled with the bliss of the absolute, when thus the truth has been seen in the heart, then this very world becomes an abode of bliss.

Attaining an unbroken flow of peace leads us to a realm beyond the mind and body, beyond even this universe of dimension and duration.

We enter the mystical state that was present before we entered this incarnation and will endure even when the body falls away.

Practice

1. Open your heart to the mystical experience and divine reunion within while you are in the process of reading, running, walking in the woods or on the beach, listening or playing music, etc.

2. Consciously be aware of the mystical experience when interacting with people and when encountering a job, success, failure or difficulty, etc.

3. Experience sustained bliss and divine reunion through prayer, *satsanga*, meditation, and self-inquiry and contemplation.

Compassionate Living

Experience the impermanence and view the world with calm benevolence

Story

In Tibetan tradition, when a person dies, the revered lama prepares the spirit, which leaves the body for three days through the seven stages of incarnation. After three days, the body becomes disposable just like everything else in the world. Then the rest of the family members and friends accompany the lama to the sacred site, typically at a top of a mountain, and watch the lama dissect the body into pieces mixed with barley flour. The lama then lights incense to call upon the white eagles for a feast... Everyone watches the process without emotion, but with simple acceptance.

Teaching

Tibetans believe the body is impermanent. Without the spirit or soul it is disposable like the food we eat and the house we inhabit, temporary and ephemeral. To practice impermanence, one shall understand that we are dying at every moment just like everything else in this ever-changing world. If we realize the nature of our temporary lives, we shall have compassion for ourselves, everyone and everything at all times. The Tibetans apply the belief to their daily living. Even at death, they wish to give their last compassion to a feast of white eagles and to contribute to the cycle of the universe, birth and death.

In yogic philosophy, there is a saying: experience 'dying before death'. So we are no longer fearful of death, the unknown, while as westerners we try every way to avoid and even to deny the concept. We live in the bubble of our existence, thinking that we are untouchable by the power of nature, a cycle of birth and death just like a tree, plant and animal. We chase dream after dream and believe our existence relies solely upon the recognition of our peers, the societal values, and even our own egocentric mind in which we have been conditioned for years and centuries, individually and collectively as whole. The cycle of death and birth is a fact at every moment of our lives, from the molecular level of the human body to the vastness of the universe. Accepting death and most importantly giving compassion to everything you do and everyone you encounter is the key of living. So the life we live in becomes meaningful from within. We start truly appreciating our existence and accepting the world as it is and ourselves as we are.

Compassion does not mean to feel pity or to condescend, but to feel with an emptying of self that would lead to an enlarged and enhanced perspective. The one and only test of a valid religious idea, doctrinal statement, spiritual experience, or devotional practice is that it must lead directly lead to practical compassion. We then understand the divine has made us kinder, more empathetic, and impelled us to express this sympathy and compassion in concrete acts of loving-kindness; it does not lead us to be unkind, belligerent, cruel, self-righteous, or even to kill. Compassion has been advocated by all the great faiths because it has been found to be the safest and surest means of attaining enlightenment. It dethrones the ego from the center of our lives and puts others there, breaking down the carapace of selfishness that holds us back from an experience of the sacred. And it gives us ecstasy, broadening our perspective and giving us a larger and more enhancing vision. As a Buddhist poem reads: "May our loving thoughts fills the whole world, above, below, across – without limit, a boundless goodwill toward the whole world, unrestricted, free of hatred and enmity."

Ancient Wisdom

Sutra 1.33: The mind becomes pure and calm by cultivating friendliness toward the happy, compassion for the unhappy, delight toward the virtuous, and benevolent indifference toward the unrighteous.

This sutra is eminently practical for maintaining the steady state while living in the world. Naturally, we must actually practice this as a discipline so that we can observe the benefit of a pervasive peaceful state while dealing with the infinite variety of people we come into contact with. We may think it would be easy to befriend the happy, delight in the virtuous, have compassion toward the unhappy and indifference toward the unrighteous, if they were strangers or distant acquaintances. But what if the unhappy or unrighteous were in our own family living in the same house, or in the workplace? Could we maintain our composure of inner steadiness beyond the familiar drama with someone we have known a long time, practice compassion and benevolent indifference toward unhappiness and unrighteousness persisting right in front of us? Consider even the same person whose moods may vary among all these qualities... can we find the right key to maintain undisturbed calm through the changes?

Consider also the case of those with whom we might have a mutual dislike. If they are happy, can we be friendly? If they are virtuous, do we take delight? Think about this. Do the practice and see what it feels like. Patanjali tells us it will be wonderful, and it will bring us to a sublime serenity.

Practice

1. Experience the cycle of the universe, birth and death, at all levels, starting from waking up in the morning to dying or sleeping at night.

2. Share appreciation of every moment of our existence within and with others through your words, deeds, thoughts and actions.

3. Experiment with the liberating concept, 'it is of no difference dying today than tomorrow', in every moment of our living. So we give our compassion to everything we do, everyone we meet, and every event we encounter.

4. Practice compassion towards those who may not be our favorite or even those who give us a difficult time. These people are our teachers who bring our consciousness into check.

5. Have compassion in ourselves and have it toward our thoughts, actions, and emotions so the world becomes the reflection of who we are.

Shambhala
Search for the sacred place

Story

Many centuries ago, his holiness the beloved Sixth Dalai Lama used to sneak out of the Potala Palace at night. He was romantic and a poet who loved to drink and sing. He wrote the most beautiful poetry in Tibet and Tibetans sing his poetry in songs today. Then one night he came to a teahouse. He started to write poetry and sing. Then suddenly he caught the glimpse of a beautiful young girl whose charm entranced him at first sight. Convinced that he had seen the *bodisattva*, the White Tara, he returned to the teahouse almost every night, very late, searching for her. She never appeared again… Then he wandered off and never returned to the palace and he died looking for her.

Teaching

That sounds like a sad story and a tragedy. Tibetans believe that finding what you are looking for is not as important as searching for it. In our contemporary culture, we are taught to be a winner on all occasions and any other compromising results would be considered failures. We are striving and expected by our peers and society to get a degree, find a partner, find a job, get married, buy a car, buy a house, have children, and maybe have aspirations to be someone.

We have become so goal-oriented that we neglect the beauty and elegance of roses and even the blades of grass along the road. Once we reach a goal we may get elated for a day, or a few days, for our 'accomplishment', and then we start chasing another goal or we feel lost about what to do next... we have completely fallen into the trap of our conditioned egotistic mind.

If we follow the ancient Tibetan way of living, we will have a joyful journey in searching for destinations and external goals of life while we sing and write poems in every moment of the day, just like the beloved Sixth Dalai Lama. We experience the life of 'here and now' and the beauty, love, kindness, and compassion residing within all manifestations of the people we meet, the events we encounter, and the thoughts and emotions we evoke. We no longer live for the future or resent what we did in the past. Every moment of our day becomes a precious moment, full of joy, where the future becomes the past. Then *shambhala*, the sacred place of enlightenment, what we have been looking for and chasing after in life – the truth, embodies us, everything and everyone.

Ancient Wisdom

Mindfulness: You are not your thoughts. Our thoughts take us away from being here now. If I am thinking about the past, or worried about the future, I am a prisoner of my thoughts. When I take a moment to observe myself having thoughts, I am no longer the thoughts. I get to be and observe at the same time. That's why, if I continue to come back to my breath, which always occurs in the here and now, it draws me into the present. And from that vantage point I can observe, as past and future attempt to draw me away from the moment. This paying attention to the here and now, to the breath, to observing one's thoughts without being critical or judgmental, is what some call Mindfulness. But what is mindfulness?

Mindfulness is a word. Nothing more, nothing less. As a word it is a symbol or a sign. As a sign or symbol it points to a way of looking at life in general and one's own life in particular. Mindfulness points one in the direction of being aware of the present moment.

Practice

1. Practice the concept of 'Buddha Time' – when people ask us, or we ask ourselves constantly during day, "What time is it?" our answer is always, "Now," so we ground ourselves in this present moment.

2. Practice the concept of 'Buddha Place' which is "Here," so we do not have to live in other places in our mind and we are right *here*.

3. Practice mindfulness in everything we do, every conscious effort we make, every word we speak, and every emotion we evoke.

4. Experience all facets of the journey in pursuing external life goals and destinations, such as excitement, sadness, success, failure, reward, and even punishment, *as it is* and *as we are*.

The Natural Bardo of Life
Embracing the transition between birth and death

Story

A powerful bandit in India, after countless successful raids, realized the terrible suffering he had been causing. He yearned for some way of atoning for what he had done. He visited a saint, to whom he said, "I am a sinner, I am in torment. What is the way out? What can I do?" The saint looked at the bandit up and down and asked him what he was good at. "Nothing," replied the bandit. "Nothing?" barked the saint. "You must be good at something!" The bandit was silent for a while, and eventually admitted, "Actually, there is one thing have a talent for, and that's stealing." The saint chuckled, "Good. That is the exact skill you will need now. Go to a quiet place and rob all your perceptions, and steal all the stars and planets in the sky, and dissolve them into the belly of emptiness, the all-encompassing space of the nature of being, the natural *bardo* of life." Within twenty-one days the bandit had realized the nature of his mind, and eventually came to be regarded as one of the great saints in India.

Teaching

In ancient times, there were extraordinary masters and students who were as receptive and single-mined as that bandit, who could, by just practicing with unswerving devotion and one single instruction, attain liberation. Even today, if we can embrace everything, everyone, and every event as opportunities for spiritual teaching, there is real a possibility that we will become enlightened.

Our minds, however, are riddled and confused. We have mistakenly identified ourselves with forms and structures that appear to be real. We then become the forms and structures as a result so that we no longer see anything, the formless and structureless, the true nature of being, in front of us and within us. To recognize the space, gap, or transition from form to formless, like birth and death, and between the completion of one situation to the onset of another is referred to as *bardo* by Tibetans.

The natural *bardo* of this life spans the entire period between birth and death. In a broader perspective, life is nothing but a perpetual fluctuation of birth, death, and transition, so *bardo* experiences are happening to us all the time and are the basic part of our psychological make-up. The deeper our sensitivity, the more acute our alertness to the amazing opportunities for radical insight offered by gaps and transitions in life for liberation.

Every moment of our experience is a *bardo*, as each thought and each emotion arises out of, and dissolves into the vastness of space, the formless state. One moment we have lost something precious, and then in the very next moment, we find ourselves resting in a deep state of peace and tranquility. When this kind of experience occurs, do not rush to make conclusions, but remain for a while in that state and allow it to be a gap, looking into the mind, so we will catch a glimpse of the deathless and formless nature of the enlightened mind. At this moment we can recognize the light and ground luminosity naturally manifested in a vast and splendid way. We then attain the liberation. That was what the bandit experienced.

Ancient Wisdom

Sutra 3.3 (*bardo* of *samadhi*): In meditation the true nature (*svarupa*) of the object shines forth, not distorted by the mind. That is *samadhi*.

In this description of *astanga yoga* we have been given several practices – *asana, pranayama, pratyahara*, etc. – but *samadhi* is not a practice. It is a shift in identity from the ephemeral corporeal self to the conscious indweller. When "that which is looking" sees the appearance, it appears in its true nature (*svarupa*) undistorted by thought, feeling or personal history. The shift to the witnessing Self is persistent; *avidya*, ego, attachment, aversion and fear have burned away in *sadhana*.

Samadhi does not mean withdrawing from the world; it only means that we see clearly that which is, without distortion from the mind. Because of the inner fulfillment in the blissful state we are no longer needy of things from the world – materially, emotionally or spiritually. We are finished with the *wheel of karma* as all our actions are performed without motive. We are happy and content, just being.

Practice

1. There are two people living in all our lives. One is the ego, the false identification of ourselves, garrulous, demanding, hysterical, calculating, and the other is the hidden spiritual being, whose still voice of wisdom you have rarely heard or attended to. So practice listening to our inner voice, our innate wisdom of discernment, and start to distinguish between the inner guidance and the various clamorous and enthralling voices of the ego.

2. A way to discover the freedom of wisdom, of egolessness, is active listening; that is, to listen and hear spiritual teaching repeatedly, and then we will be reminded of the hidden wisdom while we practice letting go of all the information, concepts, ideas, and prejudices that our heads are stuffed with.

3. Contemplate and reflect each *bardo* we experience, the transition from birth to death, and slowly unfold and enrich what we have understood intellectually, and carry that understanding and experience from our head to our heart.

4. Use meditation to deepen the experience of *bardo*, the transition from birth and death, the transition from one thought to another, one emotion to another, and one event to another.

Sound Healing

Love is truth expressed in primordial sound

Story

I was inspired by a poem, written by Sean Scheuering at age 12 at the International Sound Healing Conference in San Francisco, 2007. I feel compelled to share it with you.

When I Drum

When I drum I can hear my heart beat
I feel excitement from my head to my feet
It takes away my pain and worry
I don't feel like I'm in such a hurry.

When I am drumming I feel free
My troubles fly away from me
And it comes all the peace and love
My spirit soars just like a dove.

When I am drumming with my friends
I feel like we are family
And when we drum we sound like one
One heart, one soul, one mind.

Teaching

We all may have such an experience when we immerse ourselves in the sound of music, the sound of the ocean, the sound of a forest, the sound of birds, the sound of love, the sound of primordial *pranava OM*, and the sound of the universe. There is no OPD (other people's dramas) and not even our own in our mind. We simply feel and experience the joy and bliss.

In the ancient times and even in our contemporary culture, we use sounds to express our feelings within, to connect to other human beings, even wild living creatures, and to illicit a deep connection with the all-providing source of the universe, the consciousness or so called "Gods." We sing in a church, we chant in a *kirtan*, we croon in the shower, we hum in the woods, and we intone with all sounds of the universe, whether consciously or unconsciously. By doing this, we feel the joy and bliss for unexplained reasons.

Pranava OM is the sound of all sounds in the universe. It derives from all sounds. It exists in all sounds. The ancient rishis were intoned with and channeled the sound of the universe and passed it down to us over thousands of years. Chanting OM or even mentally humming the OM brings you a profound gratitude for life and for the abundance this universe provides us. It heals all our sorrows and sadness which cause almost all physical illnesses.

Ancient Wisdom

Sutra 1.28: *Repeat pranava OM and immerse yourself in its meaning.*

OM is called the *pranava*; from the Sanskrit root *prana*, meaning vitality, or that conscious energy flow that enlivens the body. The recommended method of practicing *pranava OM* as a sacred mantra is to repeat the first two sounds (*ah ... oh*) in passing, going almost immediately to sustain the *mmm* sound, then close it off and pause in the stillness. Repeat this silently on the in-breath and the out-breath for meditation. This practice not only displaces other thoughts in the mind but actually evokes the presence of the Self. What you feel in this presence is your true original nature.

The practice of constant repetition of the *pranava OM* is called *mantra japa*. When it is set to music in chant it is called *swadhyaya*. We see here that Patanjali is giving us yet another practice for our *sadhana*. The first practice, given in sutra 2, is restraint of *vrittis* in the mind, or meditation. The second practice (sutra 12) is *vairagya*, non-attachment. Now we have *mantra japa* to sustain our focus on the divine *purusha*.

Practice

1. Listen to the melody of a song or musical piece without using our mind to interpret the meaning of it.

2. Listen to the voice of Silence.

3. Pay attention to the pause between notes and feel the silence in them.

4. Immerse ourselves in the mystical sounds by singing and playing a music instrument.

5. Listen all the sounds surrounding you and tune them into the sound of *OM*.

6. Listen to the sounds in the room and outside, listen to the inner sounds and outer sounds, and feel the vibrations across the two ends of the sound spectrum.

Current of Divine Grace

Experience pulsation of the universe within and without

Story

There is a story about a Zen master: The master has a faithful but very naïve student who regarded him as a living Buddha. Then one day the master accidentally sat down on a needle. He screamed, "Ouch!" and jumped into the air. The student instantly lost his faith and left, saying how disappointed he was to find that his master was not fully enlightened. Otherwise, he thought, how would he jump up and scream out loud like that?

Teaching

The master was sad for his student when he realized that his student had left, and said, "Poor man! If only he had known that in reality neither I, nor the needle, nor the 'ouch' really existed." These experiences are merely *maya* – veils of the universal consciousness, like waves mistaken for the ocean, rope mistaken for a snake in the dark, the space in a bottle mistakenly considered separate from the space in the universe, and our thoughts and emotions mistakenly perceived as being what we are. Do not let us make the same impulsive mistakes as that Zen student who had fundamentally failed to discriminate between the truth and the veils of truth. What we need to learn and practice is how to change the paradigm of the thinking mind from being culturally conditioned to being free, harmonious, and compassionate.

At another level, every thought we have, every emotion we experience, every action we take, and every form in which we engage is the manifestation of the Divine herself, the Shakti energy of Siva consciousness, and the play of Divine Grace. The creation is the form of the creator, the creator is in the creation we experience every moment of the day, and the creation and creator are one. When we understand the essence of how the 'Divine play' occurs in our lives every day, we experience the current of grace flowing into us within and without. Our sorrow, sadness, stress, anxiety, disappointment, failure, success, happiness and joy are merely expressions and the play of our true Divine Self. We become one with the truth and with the flow of grace when we do not mistakenly identify ourselves as these emotions and thoughts.

Every sense of ours is a gateway to the Divine Grace and seeing the world is the embodiment of the Divinity. Supreme intelligence then expresses itself in everything and everywhere in our lives. The world becomes the embodiment of Shakti energy. We see ourselves much bigger than we are.

Ancient Wisdom

Yoga Vasistha, VI.1:93: There is in fact no reality which corresponds to the words 'world' and 'ego-sense'. Just as emptiness exists, not different from space, even so this world-appearance exists in the supreme being or infinite consciousness – whether in the same form or with another form. When thus the reality of this world is well understood, then it is realized as the supreme Self (Shiva).

When I was traveling in India a few years ago I went up to Rishikesh, in the Himalayas, at the headwaters of the Ganges River. From the ashram I wandered into town to ask directions to the Shiva temple. I noticed a saintly looking person standing on the side of the road, so I approached him to ask directions. Before I could say anything, he bowed to me and said, "Ah Shiva, you have come to me in this form." This illustrates the point of view that all appearance is simply the Divine Play of consciousness itself.

Practice

1. Experience every sense, every thought, every emotion, and every act as the play designed by the Divine.

2. Experience the full spectrum of sounds, colors, thoughts, and emotions when you sit and meditate.

3. Experience oneness in everything you do and every thought you have.

4. Experience the beauty and love that reside in every plant, every blade of grass, and every grain of sand.

You Are Bigger Than Your Egoic Self
Do not become a slave to your thoughts and emotions

Story

A modern spiritual teacher, Eckhart Tolle, told a story in his book titled *New Heaven and New Earth*: One lady who was a school teacher and in her forties was told by her physician only to have a few months to live due to her late stage of cancer. She learned to sit quietly by herself, or with Eckhart Tolle, and practiced contemplation in feeling, not in thinking. She seemed content with her condition and enjoyed 'just being' rather than 'doing' as she used to all the time in the past.

One day she was very angry and furious and she told Ekhart Tolle her precious diamond necklace was gone. It was a very special necklace and had sentimental value – it had been passed down from her grandmother. She suspected her maid who had come to clean her house had stolen it. She asked him what to do – should she confront the maid or report to the police her suspicion. He told her to contemplate a couple of questions before taking any actions: "When do you plan to let go of the diamond necklace or other possessions, because eventually we all have to physically leave this world and let go of everything we possess? Do you become less or insignificant when you do not have the diamond necklace?" After a while of contemplating, especially with the second question, she regained her quietness and her bigger Self. She even started giving away all her possessions to others and even to her maid. She became more and more radiant and the light shined through her as her physical condition regressed. After she passed away the necklace was found in the medicine cabinet. Who knows if the necklace has been stolen, misplaced, or even returned? Does that really matter?

Teaching

Our emotions are nothing but the bodily expression of our own thoughts that are deeply rooted in the roles we play, the culture we grow up with, the society we associate with, the forms we identify with, and the past experiences that have conditioned us. The emotions we experience in life, like riding a rollercoaster, walking through the forest, and surfing in the ocean, have the full spectrum of high and low, valley and peak, and rough and smooth or somewhere between.

We often identify ourselves in the spectrum of the ephemeral phenomena of the emotions with the result that we not only experience but also become the emotions of sadness, sorrow, envy, jealousy, anxiety, hatred, revenge, withdrawal, pleasure, enjoyment, satisfaction, complacency, righteousness, gratification, contentment and love. We attach to these emotions even when it is time to let go and when they no longer serve our life situation. We try to cling to and hold on to them. We are afraid to lose our identity and afraid to let go because we do not like to fall into the unknown or to lose our identification with the range of our emotions and forms.

These emotions are made out of our thoughts – the conditioned mind, the modification of forms. The attachment to the forms or the emotions is the ego. The ego identification has been imbedded in our culture and our human conditioning for thousands of years. We feel inferior when someone knows more than we do, we feel lesser when someone has more material stuff than we do, we suffer when we do not get what we want, we feel diminished when we lose 'battles' in life, we feel lost when the ego forms are threatened.

We are bigger than we think and perceive we are. We are the silence in the midst of worldly screaming and shouting. We are the formless beings manifested in all forms of life and the universe. We are the conscious indwellers residing in all unconscious speech, words, deeds and acts. We are the sentient life forms veiled in the darkness of delusive *maya*. We have been given the experience of a spiritual evolution as teachers, students, wives, husbands, spiritual aspirants, even crooks and murderers. We have been given the ability to express Divine Grace in all forms of life and all ranges of emotions.

Ancient Wisdom

Sutra 2.1: Self-discipline, study and recitation of sacred texts, and absorption in the true inner Self, constitute the essentials of yoga in action

Sutra 2.2: Practicing these essentials, we overcome the obstacles and attain *samadhi*.

Yoga *sadhana* is also known as the Path of Discrimination (*viveka*): discernment of the Self from the ego. It is through the power of *viveka* that our fundamental mistaken identity is burned away. This erroneous identification with our thoughts, feelings, body and personal history is gradually diminished through *yoga and meditation*. In the same way, we gradually become stronger in the awareness that we are the divine presence. It is not that the ego goes away, but that it becomes channeled into a positive, supportive and peaceful attitude.

The power of *sadhana* is in the practices given in this second book of *Yoga Sutras*. Through these practices *samadhi* is attained, beginning with the *niyamas* (observances) of self-discipline, study and *mantra japa*, and devotion to the Self.

Practice

1. When a person takes your shirt let the person have your coat. Think that the person needs more than you do, and practice non-attachment to the forms.

2. Accept losses in materials and from ego-battles of love and life, and practice letting go as a way to experience formlessness of the forms manifested in life.

3. Life is given to us for the experience of our spiritual evolution. Practice embracing the experiences by not attaching to and clinging, and feel the light shining through the experience and the Divine Grace flowing into the experience and our precious being.

4. When we encounter any life situation, experience 'feeling of' and not 'thinking of' the experience.

Reaction to the World
The root of suffering

Story

In the autumn of 2007, three Japanese yogis spent 10 days yoga vacationing with me at the home of SchoolYoga Institute. They were dedicated yogis wanting to experience the light of "Guru" presence and the wisdom of "Guru" teaching. One of them has claimed such an experience when she spent a month studying with me in the past and the other two are her students who have been inspired to come and experience the same.

As days went by, they experienced the spirit of living like a yogi but at the same time they became agitated, drained, and negative. By the fifth day, they came to me and verbalized their disappointment of the living and studying experienced so far: "You do not behave like a guru. The ways you expressed your emotion and some part of your life is not guru-like and very disappointing." "We did not have the experience as we expected from living here and studying with you." …

Teaching

I shared with them that the suffering they experienced had come from the reaction of the mind wanting something different than what is, had come from a discrepancy between expectation and reality, and had come from the fallacy that a "guru" should carry his students to the light of consciousness. The yogic path is a path of self-realization through self-inquiry, self-exploration of the truth, and self-discipline. The so-called "guru," or the light of wisdom, only serves as a road mark, instrument, or tool. The world is filled with dramas, wars, violence, hatreds, disappointments, likes and dislikes. We can either react by getting caught in the ocean of dramas and sufferings, or we can choose to respond to the world in a peaceful and loving way from within – because we know that we cannot change the world, the nature of impermanency. We have control of our own journey, external and internal, material and spiritual.

Buddha said whatever suffering arises has a reaction as its cause. If all reactions cease to be then there is no more suffering. One fleeting reaction of liking or disliking may not be very strong and may not give much result, but it can have a cumulative effect. The reaction is repeated moment after moment, intensifying with each repetition and developing into a craving or aversion. The mental habit of insatiable longing for 'what is not' implies an irremediable dissatisfaction with 'what is'. The stronger longing and dissatisfaction become, the deeper their influence on our thinking, our speech, and our action, and the more suffering they will cause.

Some reactions are like lines drawn on the surface of a pool of water – as soon as they are drawn they are erased. Others are lines traced on a sandy beach – if drawn in the morning they are gone by night, wiped away by the tide or the wind. Others like lines cut deeply into rock with chisel and hammer. They too will be obliterated as the rock erodes, but it may take ages for them to disappear. Throughout each day of our lives, the mind keeps generating reactions, but at the end of the month, at the end of the year, and even at the end of our lives, we shall remember the deepest impression. Such deep reactions lead to immense suffering.

Which mental actions determine our fate? If the mind consists of nothing but consciousness, perception, sensation and reaction, then which one of these gives in to suffering? Consciousness merely receives the raw data of experience as it is, perception places the data in a category, sensation signals the occurring of the previous steps. The job of the three is only to digest incoming information passively. But then the mind starts to react, passively gives way to attraction or repulsion, likes or dislikes. This reaction sets in motion a fresh chain of events.

The road we take towards emerging from such suffering is to accept 'what is', not as a philosophical concept or an article of faith, but as a fact of existence which affects each one of us in our lives. With this acceptance and an understanding of what suffering is and why we suffer, we can stop being reactionary and start responding to the world of dramas in a kind, loving, and harmonious way.

Ancient Wisdom

Gurumayi Chidvilasananda, speaking on the topic of *vairagya* (non-attachment), November 2003: "With detachment, we can be resolute regarding our life. When you are resolute, you have a mature relationship with your thoughts and feelings. It's when we're identified with our thoughts and feelings that we are puppets controlled by our own habits of reaction. With detachment from these habits of reaction, we live more in alignment with our intentions and priorities, and we are less subject to being derailed by the pull of the senses, by other people's emotions, and by unforeseen events."

Practice

1. Experience each suffering as a mental reaction to a thought, event, behavior, or action.

2. Through the experience of suffering, feel the release of the suffering by simply accepting it as it is and embrace it.

3. Experience each of the three stages of the mind – consciousness, perception, and sensation – when you encounter a thought

and event, especially the first stage. Feel that your existence is a reflection of the world.

4. Experience each suffering as derived from ourselves not from others. Then experience a peaceful way to resolve the suffering.

Emotion: Bodily Expression of Thoughts in the Mind
Bring it into the Light of Consciousness

Story

I was talking to one of my yogi friends over the phone a few nights ago. She sounded very sad and depressed and I asked why. She told me that she was in the drama of how to balance compassion and disappointment because she has committed her life to her marriage for the past but her husband has betrayed her… she was experiencing an emotional rollercoaster ride. I tried to counsel her with my own stories and all yogic techniques: 'it too shall pass', 'letting go', 'divine presence', 'compassion and cosmic love' … It seemed not to be working very well. She just kept talking and expressing her emotions for a long time. Finally she said to me, "Thanks for listening to me. I am feeling much better now." I was bewildered and wondered how it happened. She sensed my bewildered mind and said to me, "When I spoke to you, I separated my emotion from the facts. The spoken words became the witness of my emotion and I am no longer my emotion …" "Wow, profound," I replied.

Teaching

Becoming an impartial witness of our emotions and thoughts in the mind leads us to the unity of the divine source and the divine energy manifested as our emotions and thoughts. We experience the embodiment between manifested and un-manifested, materials and spirit, form and formless, and mortal and immortal selves. We are no longer controlled by the emotion but fully experience the emotions as they arise without judgment and value. We then slip into a crack of vastness, of emptiness, and flow into the glimpse of divine grace...

What is an emotion? It is the bodily expression and manifestation of the thoughts in the mind. Emotion arises when the mind and body meet. It is a bodily reaction and reflection of the mind. When we experience the emotion of sadness, depression, disappointment, fear, envy, desires and even likes and pleasure, we often become the emotion expressed in all senses of the living being. These emotions, however, are subject to the law of duality and bound to have an opposite effect sooner or later, when we identify ourselves with them. Likes become dislikes, pleasure becomes pain, and happiness becomes suffering. When our emotions are not fully experienced, watched and/or expressed as a result, we likely become unconscious of the cause. We keep creating *karma*, the cause-and-effect, and we end in the never-ending-cycle of *samara*, the suffering that Buddha referred to.

Only when we go beyond the emotions, go between the emotions, and embody the emotions do we reveal the gap, the space, and the vastness of deep reverence and deep connection with 'being' in the forms of joy, bliss, love and peace. The glimpse of the gap is often short-lived so that we seldom experience such a sensation due to mind domination and our attachment and identification with the emotions in our egoic mind. The sense of joy, love, bliss and peace are easily obscured but never can be destroyed by the unenlightened unconscious emotions in the mind, just like the clouds can overshadow the sun but never destroy the sun, the light of consciousness.

Ancient Wisdom

From a talk by Swami Vasudevananda of the Saraswati Order: As your consciousness streams into the heart again and again, you find yourself becoming more present, you arrive *here* more completely, more fully aware, more fully yourself, beyond the confines of the ego. This is what we are learning in meditation – to arrive completely here as who we truly are, with our thoughts and actions permeated by *purno'ham vimarsa*, the perfect I-consciousness.

The ego, however, has a way of appropriating thoughts and feelings and actions. It believes that it is responsible for them. And most of us have a longstanding and well-developed habit of listening to and believing what the ego tells us.

How does it come to an end, this ego story?

The practices and teachings give you many means to access your awakened inner power and to weaken the grip of the ego. One way that you practiced is to regard the various thoughts and feelings that arise in meditation as forms appearing in consciousness. As you practice this over time, you begin to gain some distance from your mental creations. In meditation you can watch thoughts and feelings arise and dissolve without needing to act on them in any way. As you release yourself from involvement in the content of your thoughts, allowing them to dissolve back into their source, your attention becomes free to rest on the one who is watching. You begin to perceive your own pure awareness and to identify with that, rather than with the creations arising within your mind. You are no longer identifying with the ego. You are meditating on your inner Self, aligning yourself with the divine power behind all your thoughts and feelings and actions. You gain a lot of inner freedom in this way.

Practice

1. Allow the emotion to be there without letting emotions control us and practice, "We are not the emotion and we are the divine presence."

2. Do not analyze – just watch and feel the energy within, a doorway to inner being, and ask the question at all times, "What is inside of me at this moment?"

3. Emotion is a bodily reflection of the mind (embodiment). Feel the sensations in the body, physiological changes, biochemical changes, and psychological changes without judgment and evaluation.

4. Bring all unconscious emotions into the light of consciousness. Practice indifference and repeat the mantra, "It too shall pass," when emotions arise.

5. Emotions arise from inside of us and need to be brought back to their origin with compassion and embodiment.

6. Emotions can be expressed impartially in conversation and journaling. We then use words as a way to watch our emotion.

7. Thinking is a small act of consciousness but consciousness exists without thinking. Do not analyze and think – simply experience how to stop analyzing and thinking.

Random Kindness
A natural expression of bliss

Story

A story comes from Ammaji's teaching: A man stood by a roadside feeling totally dejected. A passerby saw him and smiled at him. For this man, who felt devoid of all hope, abandoned by all, that one smile had a tremendous effect. The very thought that there was someone who cared enough to look at him and smile gave him renewed energy. At that moment, he remembered a friend whom he had not seen for a long time and he wrote him a letter. The friend was so happy to receive the letter that he gave ten rupees to a poor woman standing nearby. The woman went and bought a lottery ticket with the money. And wonder of wonders, she won the lottery. While walking home with her prize money, she saw a sick beggar lying on the pavement. She thought, "It is thanks to God that I received this windfall; let me use some of it to help this poor man." She took the beggar to a hospital and arranged for his treatment. When the beggar was released from the hospital, he happened to see an abandoned puppy that was cold and hungry and too weak to walk. The puppy whimpered piteously, and the beggar's heart melted. The beggar picked up and wrapped the puppy with a piece of cloth and lit a small fire by the roadside to warm him. He shared his food with the little dog, who, after all that love and care, soon regained his strength. The puppy followed the beggar. That night the beggar stopped in front of a house and asked if he could spend the night there. The family allowed him and the dog to sleep on their porch. That night, in deep sleep, the beggar and the people of the house were awakened by the incessant barking of the puppy. They discovered that the house had caught on fire – right near the child's bedroom. At the very last moment, they managed to rescue the child and, working together, they put out the fire.

So, one good turn led to another; giving shelter to the beggar and his dog saved the family. The child grew up to be a saint. Countless people found joy and peace through their association with him...

Teaching

We see that one smile, a random act of kindness, affected the lives of many people. That one small smile illuminated people's lives. Even the smallest things we do for each other can bring about a great transformation in our lives and our society. We may not be aware of it right away, but every good deed certainly bears fruits that may be manifested in different forms. We therefore shall perform acts of speech, action, and thought to enrich and to benefit others.

Our genuine kindness derives from deep-seated peace and bliss. Through our *sadhana* practices we gradually reveal the true essence of 'human being'. We start perceiving the world as a perfect place in to which to live, we start accepting the world as it is, we start receiving abundance in the world of gratitude, we start sensing the love from everywhere and from within, and we then start sending the selfless love and kindness to others as our true existence...

There is no more I and mine, no more egoic thought patterns, but a deep, serene sense of reverence for the universe, unity and harmony. No more pretending, but the natural expression of our divine, blissful Self to others in our lives. So giving compassion and love to others is no longer an obligation, but a radiation of the Divine Grace in the forms of our words, acts and deeds.

Ancient Wisdom

Sutra 2.35: When one is established in harmlessness (*ahimsa*), those near are at peace.

The virtue of *ahimsa* is not attained through practice of non-violence. This observance is born in meditation. When one becomes established in undisturbed inner peace, then harmlessness is practiced effortlessly in the world. Not only is the yogi undisturbed by provocation, but the state itself is a calming force that shines in one's company.

This principle is true of all the observances and restraints. The virtues arise in the state of the meditator and are then practiced in the world with no effort. We might say that the virtues of *yama* and *niyama* are built-in to the Self; that is its nature. All that happens in *sadhana* is that the conditioned mind gets out of the way to allow the true nature of the Self to emerge; the veil of ignorance (*avidya*) falls away. The only attainment is surrender to that which has always been our Self.

Practice

1. Provide random acts of kindness to others – a smile, a gift, genuine words, a divine act, etc. – without expecting anything in return, especially during our precious holiday seasons.

2. Cultivate and reveal the deep sense of reverence, love, peace, compassion, and bliss through our daily *sadhana* practice on and off our yoga mat. When we experience this state, the giving becomes a natural expression of our being.

3. Joyful giving is an act of instantaneous receiving in the world of abundance. Share your abundance with others in the forms of material wealth and spiritual wealth.

Connecting the Elements of the Universe
Experience the joyful bliss

Story

I had a great experience connecting the elements when I was skiing in Lake Tahoe in 2008. In the late afternoon I felt there was a drive and an urge to have a scenic spot for meditation. So I got to the top of the mountain and skied to a spot overlooking Lake Tahoe about 10,000 feet in the sky. That was an end spot for a black diamond run so not many skiers came by. I removed my ski gear and sat down facing the lake while the sun was sitting directly in front of me. I sensed everything around me, the scent of the alpine trees and snowy forest, a panoramic view of snowy mountains in a great depth of distance, a bird's view of the lake, and the sound of wind near and in the distance. They sounded like a symphony of OM... When I closed my eyes at this moment, I felt extremely blissful, experienced a joy with tears in my eyes, felt completely connected to the mountains, lake, snow, wind, ice, and myself, everything in me and outside of me... I did not want to get out of that state, and I fully experienced something extraordinary, peace, serenity, solitude, and oneness with all there is...

The rest of the day and the next day I experienced life from a bright light, no more dramas, no more worries, no more anticipation, only love, joy, and contentment...

Teaching

Everyday life brings us gradually or suddenly, whether we like or not, to the world of duties and responsibilities, needs and wants, inspirations and aspiration, likes and dislikes, joy and sadness, bliss and devastation, solitude and sufferings – do they sound familiar to you? Especially after a return from a long and joyful vacation from a tropical paradise, Marsella Beach, Nicaraqua, the reality and the duality of life slams itself in your face. I often wonder why we can't just always live in the state of joyful bliss.

Ayurveda medicine, from the life of wisdom dating back 2500 years ago in India, teaches us one of the spiritual ways to reveal ultimate health and healing. The universe composes five essential elements, fire, earth, water, air and ether. We human beings come from the five elements and when we leave this body we return to the elements. Our bodies are an integral part of the universe, so they are made out of the five elements. We all have an experience of joy and solitude when we stride along a beach, walk on a trail in the forest, swim in a lake, ski down a slope, run in the rhythm, sit around a fire, take a shower... Sometimes we wonder why we feel such a way. It is the connection we make to the universal elements from outside and from within. We feel grounded and connected to everything around us and within us. The fundamentals of the universal elements, wind, air, water, heat, fire, earth, tree, space, river, and mountains are the purest forms of our existence – no dramas, no mind interpretation, no ego, only the consciousness underlying all existence.

Ancient Wisdom

Sutra 2.17: The cause of avoidable suffering is the illusion that the seer is the same as the seen.

There is purpose in the unsteadiness of the mind; it is seeking stillness and repose. It will not rest until it finds peace. Through meditation it overcomes the restlessness and enters into the bliss of sublime contentment. Let us have a new appreciation of the torture of the mind; ultimately, attachment and fear bring us transcendence. The purpose of suffering is to create the longing for its opposite. Think about it. In your deepest hurt, don't you wish for some way out, some means to escape the suffering? We discover in meditation that it is only the ego that suffers, and we are not the ego; we are the transcendent Self that is in bliss all the time. In this way we extinguish the illusion that the seer is the same as the seen. We now know that the seer is the silent witness of the appearance. The Self, the eternal subject, awakens to the time-bound mutability of the objective appearance. The suffering is forever finished.

Practice

1. Practice 'being-aware-of-dramas' unfolding in daily life and notice the emotion that arises from the drama: "I am angry, I am elated, I am suffering, I am joyful…"

2. Practice 'watching-experiencing-dramas' unfolding in daily life and notice the sensations that arise from the physical body, mental body, psychological body, and subtle energy body without judgment and criticism. Tell ourselves that we are not those sensations and we are the impartial witness of the sensations.

3. Use the spiritual techniques to reveal our inner stillness, compassion, love and bliss to the pain and suffering; techniques such as 'accept-as-it-is', 'connect-to-elements', 'find-oneness-in-all', and 'stillness-through-meditation-asana-pranayama'.

4. Verbalizing the experience to others or writing the experience in your reflective journal is another way to witness your emotions, thought, pains, and even sufferings.

Unavoidable Dramas – Manifestation of Divine Presence
Opportunities for Liberation

Story

Once I was in a relationship with a beautiful yogini. We fell in love deeply and danced with our joy and bliss at all levels of human existence… Not too long from the experience of euphoria, her sufferings from her past and from within surfaced and brought a new twist into the relationship. She became moody and unpredictable. One moment she was in the state of bliss and another moment she was in the state of devastation. She started drifting away from the relationship while she tried to hold on to the sweetness of loving kindness of union between two ends of polarities…

As a result, my suffering was brought to the surface as well. I started experiencing the sense of loss, the sense of disappointment, sense of separation, sense of loneliness, sense of doubt in life purpose, and sense of uncertainty… I still vividly live in that moment from time to time…

Teaching

It has been a human, yet enlightening experience for me to participate in and to witness at the same time my dramas unfolding into emotion, thoughts and actions. We human beings swing from one end of the spectrum to another. We, most of the time, are not even aware of the ups and downs, peaks and valleys, ins and outs of love, sadness and joy, disappointment and fulfillment, etc. At least, I am aware of the happenings around me and within me.

Whether or not we can still follow the flow of the universe beyond the duality is dependent upon how deeply we are into our spiritual practice. Are we aware or not aware? Are we witnessing and solely participating? Are we taking actions and simply riding the waves of the ocean, like when we lose control in surfing and tumble like a washing machine. If we are not even aware, there is no witnessing and there is no action taken, which results in suffering; this has been my experience at all levels of emotion, from suffering to bliss and from desperation to unison. I sincerely cherish and fully embrace all that is happening in me and around me. As all saints and wise ones declare, love, or energy of love, is the driving force of our divine universe...

I had a conversation regarding human suffering with my yogi friend, Nancy, during my lunch break at the middle of writing this experience. She said, "Pain is inevitable but suffering is optional." The human pains that I called dramas in life are unavoidable. They are an integral part of our human existence. We believe that our pains are from external sources like parents who brought us into the world, a partner who brings us unhappiness, a boss who makes our lives miserable, a house we live in that is too small, a city we live in that is too cold, and money we make that is too meager. Most of us fail to realize that our pains directly derive from our own inner state.

When we let the human pains, individually and collectively as a human race, enter our mind, we become the pains. But...

> When we watch them like passing clouds in the blue sky,
>
> When we no longer judge the world and accept it as it is and as it appears,

When we dwell ourselves into silence and inner stillness,

When we experience oneness with the elements like trees, grass, sand, rivers, people, even emotion,

When we no longer separate ourselves from the existence of the universe,

When we experience the bliss amidst daily living,

When we connect to all the providing sources of the universal energy,

When we find peace and love in all the suffering of our egoic existence,

When we live life in profound and everlasting compassion, love and bliss,

Then the pains no longer exist and suffering becomes optional, as my dear friend said.

Ancient Wisdom

Sutra 2.17: The cause of avoidable suffering is the illusion that the seer is the same as the seen.

There is purpose in the unsteadiness of the mind; it is seeking stillness and repose. It will not rest until it finds peace. Through meditation it overcomes the restlessness and enters into the bliss of sublime contentment. Let us have a new appreciation of the torture of the mind; ultimately, attachment and fear bring us transcendence. The purpose of suffering is to create the longing for its opposite. Think about it. In your deepest hurt, don't you wish for some way out, some means to escape the suffering? We discover in meditation that it is only the ego that suffers, and we are not the ego; we are the transcendent Self that is in bliss all the time. In this way we extinguish the illusion that the seer is the same as the seen. We now know that the seer is the silent witness of the appearance. The Self, the eternal subject, awakens to the time-bound mutability of the objective appearance. The suffering is forever finished.

Practice

1. Practice 'being-aware-of-dramas' unfolding in daily life and notice the emotion that arises from the drama: "I am angry, I am elated, I am suffering, I am joyful…"

2. Practice 'watching-experiencing-dramas' unfolding in daily life and notice the sensations that arise from the physical body, mental body, psychological body, and subtle energy body without judgment and criticism. Tell ourselves that we are not those sensations and we are the impartial witness of the sensations.

3. Use the spiritual techniques to reveal our inner stillness, compassion, love and bliss to the pain and suffering; techniques such as 'accept-as-it-is', 'connect-to-elements', 'find-oneness-in-all', and 'stillness-through-meditation-asana-pranayama'.

4. Verbalizing the experience to others or writing the experience in your reflective journal is another way to witness your emotions, thought, pains, and even sufferings.

Getting Into the Zone
Living in a timeless moment

Story

A great Russian weightlifter, Yuri Vlasov, describes his experience of the zone as a "precious, white moment." At the peace of tremendous and victorious effort, with the blood pounding in your head, all suddenly becomes quiet within you. Everything seems clearer and whiter than ever before, as if a great spotlight had been turned on. At that moment you have the conviction that you contain all the power in the world, that you are capable of anything, that you have wings. There is no more precious moment in life than this, the white moment, and you will work very hard for years just to taste it again.

"It was a type of euphoria; I felt I could run all day without tiring, that I could dribble through any of their team or all of them, that I could pass through them physically. I felt I could not be hurt. It was a strange feeling of invincibility," recalled the soccer genius, Pele, in his autobiography, *My Life and the Beautiful Game*.

"I've sort of felt one with the water and my stroke and everything," recalled a swimmer.

"Everything seemed to be happening in slow motion out there. I could see what was happening in advance, and anticipate plays," recalled Jerry West, a great NBA basketball player.

"When I am in this state, the cocoon of concentration, I am living fully in the present, not moving out of it. I am aware of every inch of my swing... I'm absolutely engaged, involved in what I am doing at that particular moment..." recalled Tony Jacklin, a great British Golfer.

Bill Russell described his experience as being magical: "[P]rofound joy, acute intuition, a feeling of effortlessness in the midst of intense exertion, a sense of the action taking place in slow motion, feelings of awe and perfection, increased mastery, and self-transcendence..."

Teaching

Yes, the sense of self-transcendence is what we all experience regardless whether or not we are elite athletes or ordinary folks, when our mind is quiet, no more distractions from the world, no more wanting and desire, no more worries and seeking, no more mind, no more thoughts, no more self, no more ego... It is just there for us to experience, that we are one with everything and everyone, that we feel we flow into the pulsation of the universe...

All sages, saints, and even ordinary folks like us strive to experience a glimpse of this precious moment when we feel euphoria, invincible, untouchable, floating, flowing, auto-piloted, optimal, ecstatic, peaceful compassion, contentment and love. This moment seems very slippery and it comes and goes. It leaves us to ponder how we can get there. When we get there, how can we sustain it for a long period of time or for the rest of our lives?

Sport psychologists suggest that athletes reach the zone through visualization, progressive muscle relaxation, counseling, goal setting, concentration and even meditation. Yoga wisdom guides us to the state of *samadhi* (the state of joy and love) and *kaivalya* (liberation) by controlling the thoughts in the mind, by surrendering our actions and deeds to higher callings, by giving our hearts to the world with selfless services, and by self-inquiring of 'who am I' and 'why I am here in the universe'. Buddha showed us ways to the state of *nirvana* (enlightenment). When you seek after enlightenment, enlightenment will elude you. Yet without seeking after it, you will never realize it. To study the Buddha way is to study the Self. To study the Self is to forget the self.

Ancient Wisdom

Sutra 19: *Pratyabhijna-hrdayam* (*The Splendor of Recognition*) by Kshemaraja, from the eleventh century (Translation and commentary by Swami Shantananda): The permanent attainment of *samadhi* is established by contemplating one's identity with Consciousness, again and again, in the state following meditation, which is full of the imprints of *samadhi*.

The sage is telling us that the state of *samadhi* neither creates nor shows us anything that wasn't already present; *samadhi* simply erases any wrong notions we may have about the nature of reality. What I find most interesting in this statement is the implicit understanding that *samadhi* is a natural function of the mind. In other words, it *is* the mind – the stabilized and quiet mind – that lets go of delusion and thereby attains the state of *samadhi*. It is the mind that experiences itself as the Self. It is the mind that realizes its own identity with the Self. A purified mind is the mirror on which Siva reflects his perfect light, the light that brims with his overflowing bliss.

We are all able to be in this state and to learn how to remain in it in the same way we might develop any skill or mental ability. We develop the capacity to remain in the state of *samadhi*, Kshemaraja tells us, by returning to the imprint that our experiences of *samadhi* have left on our waking consciousness in the state we're in following meditation – in other words, by dwelling on the memory of any glimpse of *samadhi* we may have had and by returning to our memory of it again and again.

Practice

1. Suspend your thoughts and dramas by paying attention to the task at hand.

2. Pay attention to every sensation that arises in the body and be fully present with that sensation without interpretation or judgment.

3. Pay attention to the thoughts and emotions in the mind and be fully present with them, and experience the bodily responses to these thoughts and emotions.

4. Go for a walk, play a sport, or take a yoga class and be present with every moment with which you are engaging, and experience the joy and even the zone from an ordinary activity.

5. Explore a balance between effort and surrender; experience the effort that sets our intention as a signpost to the optimal state, and the surrender of letting go of all the expectation and desires.

Luminous Being
Leave nothing behind

Story

I felt like an eagle soaring through the sky, soaring through the universe, and soaring through a cosmic plane, soaring through every part of my existence, effortlessly with a simple flip of the wings. From a bird's point of view, the life on earth and in my literal existence becomes nothing but the spectacle of perspectives. The life no longer has past or future, and the past and future become extensions of presence; there is no attachment to the duties and responsibilities; there is no more dwelling on past relationships; there is no resentment and no regret for my existence; there is no plan for the future; and there is no unfinished business to complete in this very life on earth… I felt like a luminous being soaring through the spectrum of the unknown.

Teaching

According to the Peruvian Shamanic healing tradition, when we leave our bodies and merge into the spirit world, we may be trapped in the lower worlds with unfinished business on earth or we may enter into the fifth world, the world of spirits. In the spirit world, we are the angels, healers, saints, rishis, even avatars. We have completed all of our businesses on earth. We become the light and the spirit of every literal existence on earth – rock, grass, desert, sand, ocean, bird, animal, river, forest, and even human beings. We soar through our lives with ease, light, beauty, and love as a luminous being. In the luminous light there is no more shadow and darkness inside and outside of us.

In the Buddhist tradition, the concept of *bardo* prepares us to die in every moment of life without resentment and regret and without unfinished business so we do not have to be caught in the between-the-worlds, the suffering and Buddhahood. In the Hindu tradition, how we learn to end suffering and duality is by finishing our karma and creating no more karma in life so we do not have to be back here on the earth to take another body to experience the suffering and duality.

Ancient Wisdom

A Sufi master once wrote: "You get two things in life – that which you love and that which you hate." Dissolution of ego and liberation from attachment and avoidance brings to an end all karma associated with things you love and things you hate. We sentenced ourselves to this incarnation to finish with what we loved and hated in previous incarnations. Seeds of karma are sewn out of strong opinions, so one of the things we are here to finish with is our opinions.

We have come back to finish with many things. All of our significant relationships are hanging there, waiting to be finished. Don't be afraid to just let go. Even new relationships come to us in order to be released. Honor the process, play it out, and let it go. Even our present physical circumstances have manifested out of previous desires. Continuing to desire a particular circumstance will bring us back to have it again.

We must take inventory of what our predominant focus of attention is on and understand the profundity of the consequence of this focus. If there is even the slightest clutching on to things of the ephemeral realm as we merge into the beyond, then around we go again. Letting go of everything every moment frees us in the present and frees us in eternity.

Disentangling from the world does not have to be a painful process. It does not require severe austerity or penance. It is not like pulling out your own teeth or hacking off your leg. Once the inner wellspring of love is tasted, we see that everything we ever craved in the world flows abundantly from within. There is a natural turning to face the source of perpetual sweetness of serenity. In this turning toward the light, there is a pliant relenting of our grip on things and relationships that once held us in thrall. As we drink in the nectar of the Soul, we gradually forget the importance of our attachments. *They* release *us* as we embrace the love and wisdom of our own inner Self.

Practice

1. Finish everything that is unfinished in everyday chores.
2. Finish everything that is unfinished in our lives.
3. Learn to resolve the unfinished business with others in love and compassion and with peace of mind.
4. Ask yourself at the end of day whether you are ready to die without regret, resentment, and unfinished business.

Shedding Shadows
Reveal the Golden Nature in Self

Story

Once upon a time, a traveler came upon a beggar sitting on a box at the roadside. A year later, when the traveler came across the same road again, here was the beggar who sat at the same place and on the same box, who was only thinner. The following year, the traveler came across the same road again, and the beggar was still at the same spot and sat on the same box but he was too weak to beg for food. The traveler stopped and asked the beggar what was inside of the box he sat on. "Nothing! I have been sitting on the same box as long as I can remember," responded the beggar. "Open it," requested the traveler. They tried and tried to open it but it was too stubborn. Finally, they opened it with a shock – a box of gold...

Teaching

We live in this world thinking that we are poor, unhealthy, unloved, alone, no food, no money, no joy, no happiness, no perfect companionship, and the list goes on. We have all these shadows and layers of conditioned habitual existence. We complain about our jobs, our dissatisfactory relationships, blame our misfortunes on others' doing, resent our past, worry about our future, and are uneasy about the unknown. We do not realize that we are sitting on a box of gold. We do not recognize that we are the resource of happiness, joy, love, wealth, and abundance.

As soon as we start shedding layers of our shadows and the illusory and unconscious self, as soon as we start realizing who we are, not as the illusory self, then we emerge into who we truly are. We then find the light that guides us and leads us to our golden Buddha nature that is full of joy and love. Recognizing the shadows can be tricky at the beginning but it becomes a beacon to resolve all the misery of our sufferings in life.

Ancient Wisdom

The Philosophy of the Panchadasi, by Swami Krishnananda (from "Discrimination of Reality, Analysis of the Self"): Through careful psychological analysis, it is observable that the love which people have for things outside is the outcome of a confused mixing up of the bliss of the Self with the changing names and forms that make up what we call the world. Hence, in loving an object, the confused mind attaches itself to the changing names and forms in its ignorance and the false notion that its love is deposited in the objects, while in truth it is in the Self, and even when we love objects we are unwittingly loving the universal Self. Hence the Self is Supreme Bliss, which is the only natural condition of spiritual existence, while all other conditions with which it associates itself are transitory phenomena, and unnatural.

From the above it would be clear that the Self eternally exists as consciousness and is absolute bliss. It is *sat-chit-ananda,* a fact that is demonstrated both by reason and intuition. The identity of the Self with the Absolute Being is declared in the *vedanta* texts, such as the *Upanishads,* which are also established by reason. But this Self is not seen, it is not visible to the eyes, hence all the misery of individual existence. Nor can it be said that it is entirely invisible, else there would be no love or pleasure. That there is a faint recognition of the existence of the *atman* is proved beyond doubt by the unparalleled affection which one has toward one's inner Self. But it is also true that it is not properly seen or known; otherwise, one would not be clinging to objects, the perishable forms of the world, which have neither reality in them nor the happiness which one is seeking. Thus there is a peculiar situation in which we find ourselves where we seem to know it, and yet not know it. There is a muddle of intelligence and torpidity of understanding, due to which there is a perpetually disturbed feeling and distracted knowledge. It is that which is responsible for our partially evincing love for ourselves and partially clinging to things that perish. The beauty and the joy are not in things but in the Self. And this is not known. It is falsely imagined to be in objects; hence the attachment that we cherish in regard to them.

Practice

1. Practice the 4 R's in shedding the layers of shadows as follows:

2. Recognize the layers of our shadows in life, such as likes, dislikes, judgment, and any unconscious acts or behaviors.

3. Refrain from reactive behavior by creating a circle around the shadows through the means of yogic and spiritual skills such as breathing, meditation, observing, etc.

4. Relax all of your tension into the love of ocean and love of mountains.

5. Resolve all of the shadows one piece at a time without judgment.

"Buy a Ticket"
Finding a balance between Divine Grace and free will

Story

There is an old Italian story about a poor man who goes to church every day and prays before the stature of a great saint, begging, "Dear saint – please, please, please … give me the grace to win the lottery." This lament goes on for months. Finally the exasperated stature comes to life, looks down at the begging man and says in weary disgust, "My son – please, please, please … buy a ticket."

Teaching

One of my students in his weekly journal wrote, "Everything has been going great except for one thing – I have lost all motivation for school and it doesn't seem important any more. My view on life and living have been flipped and reversed after some of the insights I've taken from this class and others along with my experiences. Normally I would get stressed if I had a paper or a project due but I don't care that much. Everything else I feel is great, showing my love to my wife just happens instead of me thinking about it and it just flows from my heart to my friends…"

Be content with what we have, be happy with what we do, be joyous with the world around us, and be present with 'what is'. This is wisdom of our spiritual practices: neither lose interest in life nor dwell in the mundane of our life. We have to remember there are duties and responsibilities and inner callings for us to live in this world and to fulfill the true destiny that we are born to do here in this very life. It may demand us, for example, to go to work, get married, go to school, raise a family, or even renounce the world. We have to respond to the true calling, our destiny, in full enthusiasm so we can live life fully and joyfully...

Destiny is a play between Divine Grace and willful self-effort. Half of it we have no control over and the other half is absolutely in our hands. Our actions yield measurable consequences when we surrender to the flow of the Divine Grace. Destiny is a process in finding a balance between living in the manifested material world and the unmanifested world of spirituality. We are the two-in-one apparatus. We are the spiritual beings coincidentally trapped in this physical body for the sole purpose of evolution, individually and collectively. We are neither entirely a puppet of the divine consciousness, nor are we the captain of our own destiny. We downhill-ski through our lives like a skier balancing on two speeding side-by-side skis – one foot on the ski called "fate or Divine Grace," the other one the ski called "free will or willful effort." The question we have to ask ourselves everyday is, "Which ski is which? Which ski do we need to slowdown or speed up to find a balance, and which ski is not under our control, which do we need to steer with concentrated effort?"

There is so much about our fate that we cannot control, but other things do fall under our jurisdiction. There are certain lottery tickets we can choose to buy, thereby increasing our odds of finding contentment. We can decide how we spend our time, with whom we interact, and with whom we share our lives and energies. We can select what we eat, read and study. We can choose how we are going to regard unfortunate circumstances in our lives – whether we see them as curses or opportunities – so we can rise above to the most optimistic viewpoint. We can choose our words, the tone of voice in which we speak to others, and most of all, we can choose our thoughts. We need to learn how to select our thoughts just the same way we select what clothes we're going to wear every day. This is the power we can cultivate to fulfill the inner calling – our true destiny.

Ancient Wisdom

The Inner Yoga of Happiness ("Destiny and Purpose"): Destiny, then, is what we create for ourselves through karma, and free will is our choice of inner composure as we go through it. But what about purpose; what are we doing here? Why are we going through all this? What is our purpose in life?

Our purpose, now, is to overcome this ignorance and rediscover the divine presence within, which has been there all the time. We see here that our life's purpose is to awaken to the Self and become established in that transcendent state of steady wisdom. This brings the end of suffering.

Practice

1. Reveal our inner calling, our destiny, through stillness of mind when we meditate, practice yoga, walk on the beach or in a forest, or even while we contemplate the mundane of everyday life.

2. Dare to take action when there is clarity in what to do with life or even a simple task like what to eat. Most of the time we have to go beyond our logical mind.

3. "Buy a ticket" if we want to win a lottery and want to embark on our chosen journey and path. So meditate, contemplate, and 'realize' in every thought and action.

4. Be watchful of our thoughts, emotions, dramas, actions, and even energetic waves, and use them as opportunities to grow and to connect our spiritual beings with our sentient beings.

Ritual

A signpost on the path of liberation

Story

Once upon a time, a great saint in India was always surrounded in his ashram by loyal devotees. For hours a day, the saint and his followers would meditate on God. The only problem was that the saint had a young cat, an annoying creature, who used to walk through the temple meowing and purring and bothering everyone during meditation. So the saint, in all his practical wisdom, commanded that the cat be tied to a pole outside for a few hours a day, only during meditation, so as not to disturb anyone. This became a habit, tying the cat to the pole and then meditating on God. As years passed, the habit hardened into religious ritual. Nobody could meditate unless the cat was tied to the pole first. Then one day the cat died. The saint's followers were panic-stricken. It was a major religious crisis. How could they meditate now without a cat to tie to a pole? How would they reach God?

Teaching

In their minds, the cat had become the means to reach God. As a spiritual aspirant we have to be cautionary when we are on our spiritual path, warns this tale, not to get too obsessed with the repetitions of religious ritual just for its own sake – especially in this divided world where the Taliban and the Christian Coalition continue to fight out their international trademark war over who owns the rights to the word God and who has the proper rituals to reach that God. In the history of humanity, there have been continuous fights and wars in the name of God, causing human suffering from bloodshed to mental illness and hatred. It still confronts us in our everyday lives – debating, arguing, and fighting about who has the righteous God and which path is the true path that leads to heaven or liberation…

Yoga teaches us there are no right or wrong ways toward God. Paths are many and the truth only has one. There are so many different ways to reach the peak of a mountain, hiking, climbing, driving, and even flying. But the experience on the top of the mountain is the same even though the journeys we embark on are completely different. We are different sentient beings and have different temperaments, so we approach our lives and even reach to our inner God differently. Who is right and who is wrong in a duty of service to humanity? Who has a better or worse job in a duty of service to our higher consciousness? We are all equal in the name of God and the universal consciousness. Diversity is in Unity.

When we experience God or the universal consciousness manifested in the forms of love, compassion, serenity and equanimity, rituals, religions, spiritual paths, and even the mundane of everyday life, they only serve as means, vehicles, conduits, and road maps. We become dogmatic when we use the means as the end and use the means to judge others. It is only a mental exercise or a philosophical inquiry when we try to understand God and the universal consciousness though our limited and conditioned intellectual minds. Awakening to the universal consciousness reveals that all the forms we experience in life, including the rituals, are temporary and subject to change, and beyond the forms there lies the formlessness of the universal consciousness.

Ancient Wisdom

Sutra 4.26: The mind, inclined toward discriminative knowledge, gravitates toward the state of liberation.

The inclination toward discriminative knowledge likely began many lifetimes ago – turning inward, overcoming outer-directed tendencies, acquiring much new learning and diligent practice of austerities. Persistence of this little-traveled path has brought us here to a steady progression toward the state of liberation.

There comes a point when more thinking about it only keeps us from it, and knowing about it, is not it. We must only be aware of just being. In this state of awareness, a marvelous thing happens.

We typically divide our awareness into two domains: the outer (objects in the appearance) and inner (thoughts, feelings and personal history). Absorbed in the Knower, the mind and its contents shift to the outer domain of appearance; then there is just impartial awareness enjoying the play against the background of stillness from which the play arises.

Practice

1. Learn to accept others' different ways of living and different ways of approaching spirituality.
2. Learn to see the beauty and love in all sentient beings, especially those who are not on the same path as we embark upon.
3. Try to experience different rituals in life and experience the truth from different paths.
4. Foster inner connection to our divine Self and the universal consciousness through our personal practice in certain rituals or spiritual paths.

The Middle Path

Neither looking to the left nor looking to the right

Story

Saraha, the founder of Buddhist *tantra*, was born to a very learned Brahmin family whose father served in the King's court. Saraha was the youngest, the brightest, and the most intelligent among his five siblings. He naturally evolved to be a great *vedic* scholar. Saraha's fame and knowledge was spreading all over the country and even the king was enchanted by him, willing to give his own daughter in marriage to him. But Saraha decided to renounce everything to become a *sannyasin*, a wandering spiritual seeker.

Saraha became a *sannyasin* and a disciple of Sri Kirti in the direct lineage of Buddha, where the Buddha had just left and the vibration and the fragrance of the Buddha was vividly experienced. "Forget about all your Vedas, all your learning, and all that nonsense," said Sri Kirti in the very first lesson. You can escape from the kingdom, you can go to Himalayas caves, you can distribute your wealth, but how can you renounce your knowledge? It is painful to become innocent like a child. But he was ready and erased all that he had known. He became a great meditator and a great scholar in the Buddhist tradition. People started coming from far away just to have a glimpse of this young man who had become so innocent, like a fresh leaf, like dewdrops on the grass in the morning...

One day, while Saraha was meditating, he had a vision of a woman in the marketplace who was going to be his real teacher even though Sri Kirti had just put him on the path. He left with Sri Kirti's blessings. He went to the marketplace and to his surprise he found the woman he had seen in the vision, and she was making an arrow. She was a young woman, very alive, earthly beautiful, and radiant with life, and she was cutting an arrow shaft, looking neither left or right, but wholly absorbed into making the arrow. As Saraha watched carefully, the arrow completed, the woman closed one eye and opened the other, and assumed the posture of aiming at an invisible target and aiming at something unknown…

Saraha started sensing an inner message from what she was doing and asked the woman whether she was a professional arrowsmith. The woman laughed and laughed, and said, "You ignorant Brahmin! You have left Vedas, but you are worshiping Buddha's sayings. So what is the point? You have changed your books, you have changed your philosophy, but you still remain the ignorant man…"

Teaching

The more knowledge we learn and the more conditioned mind we engrain, the more plastic and the more artificial we become. Sri Kirti was a great philosopher, and while Saraha had dropped all his learning, the Vedas and scriptures, he was still a learned man and had his own scripture and his own Vedas. Even though he was anti-philosophical, the way of his practice was a philosophy in its own right. Her laugh indicates that Buddha's teaching can only be known through action and experience, not through words or books.

Neither looking to the left nor to the right, we see her just looking in the middle while she is making an arrow. We are like a pendulum moving from left to right and from right to left, but the middle of pendulum is where we all experience centeredness and stillness in the midst of the extremes in our lives through appearances of left and right. Buddha says, to be worldly is to be worldly, and to be otherworldly is also to be worldly, to worship money, fame and even knowledge, or to be against them, is to be unworldly and unconscious, to seek power is foolish or to escape from it is also foolish. Just to be in the middle is the wisdom of Buddha teaching.

To be total in action is free from action. *Karma* is created when we are not totally in our acts because they leave traces in our cosmic beings. So do everything in full attention and leave no trace to be carried into our lives, creating *karma*. Any hangovers remain with you like a ghost. Our eyes are clear of the past and our vision of the future is not clouded. In that clarity we come to know the reality and the truth.

Ancient Wisdom

Yoga Sutras (from the introduction): Throughout the book we are reminded of two fundamental practices that lead to the final state, *kaivalya* (liberation). One practice is *vairagya* (dispassion, non-attachment) and the other is *viveka* (discrimination). In life, everything comes to us and everything leaves us. In both pleasure and pain we can welcome whatever comes, and release whatever leaves us. In the practice of *vairagya* we not only let go completely when it is time, but we do not become attached in the first place to whatever comes to us in the river of abundance.

Practice

1. Immerse ourselves in everything we do and think so we do not create any more karma in our lives.

2. If there is unfinished business, surrender it to the source of the universal consciousness so no karma is created.

3. Let go of all learned knowledge that helps us live in the manifested material world when we try to connect the spirit of our essential existence.

4. Find and reveal the middle path in everything we do and every act we make.

Dreaming into Being
Working on the level of Eagle, beyond the level of Serpent

Story

A traveler comes across two stonecutters. He asks the first, "What are you doing?" and receives a reply unhappily, "Squaring the stone." He then walks over to the second stonecutter and asks, "What are you doing?" and receives a reply with a big smile, "I am building a cathedral."

Teaching

Both workers are performing the same task, but one of them is aware that he has the choice to be a part of a great dream. "To dream into being" is a yogic and shamanic way of living in this literal world. We can either live on the level of our senses like serpents moving through jungle to search for food and escape from dangers, or we can live like an eagle, visioning the world from above in a timeless fashion and connecting our actions and thoughts into being, a deeper meaning of our lives.

Most of the time, we are trapped in this literal world of instinct, survival, and the dramas of our mind and emotions. We live in search of food, shelter, money, status, a partner, and security. Fulfilling the expectations of society, others, and even ourselves leads us on the level of physical and emotional existence. When we are hungry we reach out for a Big-Mac to satisfy our sense craving. When we are sick we get pills to settle the physical and emotional senses of illness. When we are not happy we grab anti-depressants to hope for a release of the emotional condition. We operate on the level of physical and mental spheres.

We do not realize that everything that happens has a higher meaning beyond the forms and conditions. Sickness may bring us a heightened alertness in connecting our soul and spirit that serves us beyond the physical and mental state. The sensation of hunger may lead to the sense of oneness that connects every sentient being. The sense of unhappiness may guide us to shine the light of consciousness on the shadows and the *karmas* that have been accumulated in the past. So life itself is no longer a chore or a task, but a process of conscious evolution for the sentient beings, as individuals or collectively as a whole. We then start dreaming into the light our literal existence.

Ancient Wisdom

Sutra 1.49: Truth of direct knowing (that is, intuition) is different from deductive reasoning or inference.

Intuition is not an uncommon experience, but we know it is a special case. It is through meditation that we fine-tune our ability to evoke this great state of truth. As we glimpse the inner stillness time and time again, a momentum grows that wells up in our being and we begin to see with new eyes. We are not so quick to analyze everything to death but can wait patiently for the essence of the appearance to emerge in the stillness. Our intention to do this is the best way to overcome the inertia of conditioned *samskaras*, and will bring the light of truth to every minute of the day. It is here that knowledge becomes wisdom.

Practice

1. Contemplate that everything happens in life has a spiritual meaning beyond our sensory and mental experience.

2. Connect to the deeper meaning of our act, behavior, thought, and emotion.

3. Experience a higher purpose of life through the midst of daily chores.

4. Take every sensation of the body, every thought of the mind, and every state of emotion as an opportunity to dream into being the conscious sentient being, the *jivanmukta*.

Art of Living

Living life half full rather than half empty

Story

A mother sent her son with an empty bottle and a ten-rupee note to buy some oil from the nearby shop. The boy went and had the bottle filled, but as he was returning he fell down and dropped the bottle. Before he could pick it up, half of the oil spilled out. Finding the bottle half empty, he came back to his mother crying, "Oh I lost half the oil! I lost half the oil!" He was very sad.

The mother sent another son with another bottle and another ten-rupee note. He also had the bottle filled, and while returning fell down, dropped the bottle, and picked up the bottle with only half the oil left. "Mother, Mother, I am so happy that I saved half the oil when I fell down," he said.

The mother sent the third son with another bottle and a ten-rupee note. Again, he filled up the bottle, fell down while returning and only picked up half the oil. He came home a bit late with a full bottle of oil. "Mother!" he said, "I was very happy to save half the oil when I fell down. But I went back to the store and helped clean the store and earned 5 rupees so I filled the bottle."

Teaching

We become unhappy when we have misfortunes. We become sad when our desire, craving, likes and dislikes are not met. We complain about everything in life that is not fair… We sit here and complain and complain while the world goes by with a pessimistic view. Some of us seem ok with everything in life and accept the world as it comes and at the same time wish that we could have more money, a bigger house, more vacation time, and be much happier, but we fail to take any action to change the situations.

The third boy is a *jivamukti* boy – no pessimism, not only of optimism, but also realism. He realizes his duty, responsibility, and *dharma* in life and tries his best to fulfill them with joy and happiness. Living in this world and in this physical body while experiencing liberation is why we are born and why we are here – to serve humanity.

Ancient Wisdom

The Philosophy of the Panchadasi, by Swami Krishnananda, "Becoming Jivanmukti": The state of *jivanmukti* is one in which desires cannot have any place because the *jivanmukta* is in a definite condition, wherein established, he practices spontaneously the law of the Absolute. All desire in the world is selfish, because it is always connected with something that is expected to bring personal satisfaction, even if others are to be deprived of their desires in this attempt. Moreover, desire is directed to something, to the exclusion of something else. Hence desire is not universal. But a *jivanmukta* is a universal person, inasmuch as his consciousness is attuned to *brahman*. For him the law of the world is the law of the Absolute, and so it is impossible for him to act wrongly, or cherish personal desires. Goodness, virtue, etc., which are qualities that a seeker aspires to possess by an effort on his part, become spontaneous expressions of a liberated soul, for the simple fact that his soul is the Soul of all beings.

Practice

1. Experience living life half full rather than half empty when we encounter our daily tasks, thoughts, and emotions.

2. Experience life situations as opportunities for us to learn and to grow from this very ephemeral phenomenon of our existence.

3. Experience every duty and responsibility fully with enthusiasm regardless of our likes and dislikes. This is our *dharma*.

4. Reveal your inner passion for life and dare to take action to change the current life situations.

Senses of Non-Duality
Experience life fully

Story

There lived a *sadhu* near where Bombay, India is now located. A very saintly man, all who met him revered him for his purity of mind, and many claimed that he must be fully liberated. Hearing himself described in such high terms, he naturally started to wonder, "Perhaps I am in fact fully liberated." But being an honest person, he examined himself carefully and found that there were still traces of impurities in his mind. Surely, as long as the impurities remain, he could not have reached the stage of perfect saintliness. So he started asking those who came to pay respects to him, "Is there anyone in the world today who is known to be fully liberated?" "Oh Yes Sir, there is the monk Gotama, called Buddha, who teaches the technique by which one can achieve liberation."

"I must go to this man and learn from him the way to become fully liberated," he stated and walked from Bombay across all of central India and came to Savatthi in northern India, where Buddha's meditation center was located. There he saw a monk going from house to house to beg for food. The wonderful atmosphere of peace and harmony was surrounding this person. The *sadhu* was convinced that he must be the Buddha, and so asked him, "I do not have much time left for my life and I want you to teach me the technique of becoming liberated."

"In your seeing, there should be only seeing, in your hearing nothing but hearing, in your smelling, tasting, touching, nothing but smelling, tasting, touching, in your cognizing, nothing but cognizing," Buddha replied. Within a few minutes, he attained the final goal of life, full liberation.

Teaching

Bodily sensations are the great gateways and portals to access our inner stillness. This is why we are still living in and experiencing our bodies as human beings. When we fully integrate our perception into sensory experiences we come to the state of joy and beauty regardless of what we do and what we think. We all have a similar experience. For example, before we eat we start to sense the aroma of food, colors of food, the full-bodied taste of food, and the texture of food, and we then reach the state of satisfaction from the process of experiencing the food; or, when we have the same food but we eat on the run or while we are angry, does the food provide you the same satisfaction?

The Buddha teaches us that when we live life through our sensory experience, there shall be no evaluation and no conditioned perception. Once our preconceived perception starts evaluating our experiences as good or bad, we see the world in a distorted way and fall into dualistic living. In order to free the mind from all conditioning, we must learn to stop judging and evaluating on the basis of past experience and even the knowledge we learned, simply to be aware of awareness taking place from within and without, without judging and reacting. Through sensory experiences, on a spiritual path we see the oneness in all and in everything, then we all become liberated, according to Buddha.

Ancient Wisdom

The core of *astanga yoga* is the eight limbs. The first four limbs (*yama*, *niyama*, *asana* and *pranayama*) are the outer practices. The final four (*pratyahara*, *dharana*, *dhyana* and *samadhi*) are the inner practices. The first of these inner practices is *pratyahara*, the withdrawal of the senses.

Sutra 2.54: When the mind is withdrawn from sense-objects, the sense-organs also withdraw themselves from their respective objects and thus are said to imitate the mind. This is known as *pratyahara*.

The senses are slaves to the mind and go wherever the mind directs. If the mind is fascinated with the contents of awareness, the senses reach out into the appearance and bring the mind all the juice the mind has an appetite for. If the mind turns inward, becomes quiet and directs its gaze to the joyous equanimity of just breathing in and breathing out, the senses also become quiet. So we see here that *pratyahara* is the mind withdrawing from external stimulation and focusing on the inner landscape; thus the senses likewise become withdrawn.

As a practical matter we can't always sit cross-legged in the dark, breathing in the bliss, but we can remain centered in the inner quiet as we live our life. *Pratyahara* can be cultivated so that the senses are not such a distraction when we are focused on the task at hand.

Practice

1. Experience food in front of us fully without judging and without any other tasks at hand or in the mind.
2. Experience walking simply for the sake of walking, the rhythm of steps, muscle exertion and relaxation, heat from the body, heartbeats, breathing...

3. Experience thinking for the sake of thinking, without judging and evaluating the thoughts that arise. It can be a bit tricky because of the complexity of the mind.

4. Experience washing dishes for the sensations of water, soap, and the texture of dishes...

5. Experience the sensations that arise when we do yoga, meditate, and contemplate without judgment from our egoic mind.

6. Then there arises the sense of awe, joy, aha, love, serenity, contentment...

Love 'n' Light
The original source of creation

Story

I had a profound, ecstatic experience when I was in the deep conscious level of spiritual light, the original source of creation. I sensed nothing but the light when the body dissolved, the senses disappeared, the mind drifted away, the emotion no longer held energy, and when duality in the universe ceased to exist. I held that state and walked outside, sitting next to a pond. Everything in the world around me was absolutely still and vast, two loving ducks swam over next to me, turned their heads, and gave me a wink, a hummingbird flew across the sky in front of me, paused in the sky and sent me a hey, the calm and tranquil pond mirrored me with its love and light, while a gentle breeze touched autumn leaves and made me cry, cry and cry… At that moment I became the autumn, became the joy, became the love, became the light, became one with all… The rest of the day and the rest of the night, I experienced nothing but the love and light.

Teaching

There is no shadow and suffering in the universe or in our human race. We are created in the light of consciousness, in the void where everything is manifested. When our body, senses of organs, energy of emotions, and thoughts of mind fall away at the time of death, we fall back or forward to the grace, the light, the love, and the light of consciousness. Where we were created is the same place where we will return. At the place of creation there is nothing but light, there is nothing but grace, there is nothing but oneness, there is no suffering, there is no drama, there is no illness, and there is no duality. All our dramas and sufferings are created by ourselves, and at the same time we all can create, become, and be the beauty, love and compassion of the conscious light in this very life.

There is no *karma* or incarnation of the past, which leads us to believe or explain our own sufferings. It is also a creation of our mind. It is quite a revolution from our traditional Eastern belief system. We humans create our own dramas, sufferings, and shadows. Ponder this. The truth is that our personal experiences always lead us to the same deep, dark hole of human collective sufferings. For what points or what reasons do we have to experience such pain and suffering if we can experience and have the choice to experience the love and light in our existence?

We can stay at the level of the light, the light of consciousness. I do not have to engage deep into human suffering and drama. We can always experience the light at the high vibratory energy, as needed, to bring the light to dispel the shadows and suffering. So we do not have to go down the road of human suffering anymore; instead, we stay at the high level of spiritual light and love and bring that light to our thoughts, words, actions, emotions, and everyday life.

If there are human lessons we need to learn, then we need to step into, or experience, the shadows of the human race and ourselves. But we do not have to experience this drama and suffering anymore. It has been enough for all of us at some point in our lives. We can just experience the light and love. Is it possible? Absolutely, but you have to verify the truth through you own experience and experimentation.

If we all came from the light, the original source of creation, there is no duality, there is no feminine and masculine, there is no separation, there is no you and me, there are no break-ups, there is no suffering, there are no dramas, there is no disease, there is no such thing as a bad place... they are call creations of our own. Experience these truth through your heart and it will take us to the land of grace and spiritual revelation.

Ancient Wisdom

Ishvara-pratyabhijna-vivrti-vimarshini, by Abhinavagupta, 10th century (p. 710): Nothing perceived is independent of perception, and perception differs not from the perceiver; therefore, the perceived universe is nothing but the perceiver.

Practice

1. Try to experience the high level of spiritual light, the light of consciousness, a newly revealed phenomenon, for a day, a week, a moon cycle as a part of your experiment.

2. Be watchful and observant of your thoughts, emotions and actions. When you sense the suffering and drama of human experience, tell yourself, "No, no, you are not going down that road."

3. Choose the words, thoughts and actions that have a high energy of spiritual vibration, such as compassion, love, light, grace, joy, abundance ... as an integral part of your everyday life.

4. Self-inquiry – Who am I? Where did I come from? Where am I going after this life? From where did this thought and emotion arise?

Walking in Beauty
In a sacred way and in each and every day

Story

Today I taught my first restorative yoga class at I AM YOGA studio. It was a profound experience. By the end of the class, my eyes filled with tears and my heart filled with reverence and love... I set the intention at the beginning of the class to have everyone experience the concept of 'Walking Beauty' and invoked the place and everyone into the sacred healing space to experience each element of the universe. I started the class by reciting the "Walk in Beauty" song:

> May you walk in beauty in a sacred way,
> May you walk in beauty each and every day,
> May the beauty of the fire lift your spirit higher,
> May the beauty of the earth fill your heart with mirth,
> May the beauty of the rain wash away your pain,
> May the beauty of the sky teach your mind to fly.

I started the class with a gentle *pranayama* and a gentle sit posture sequence. Then I used five restorative postures with props to invoke the five elements of the universe. With each chakra I took them on middle-world journey to the earth (first chakra), the water (the second chakra), the fire (the third chakra), and the fire (fourth chakra) to experience the qualities of each element and what lessons we learn from them. Finally, we lay down in *sivasana* to experience the last three chakras in the element of space, the vast emptiness of space, the loving and divine light, before being called back to the reality to experience the beauty of the universe with our full senses.

Teaching

Every day is a beautiful day, every thought is a beautiful thought, every word we speak is a beautiful word, and every step we take is a beautiful path. This is the way of walking in beauty – the native indigenous people lived in this sacred way, and in each and every day, for thousands of years. When we live in beauty, we experience the beauty; when we live in joy, we experience the joy; when we live in love, we experience the love; when we live in grace, we experience the grace. This is the walk in beauty.

When the beauty of the fire radiates in our hearts, it lifts our spirits higher. The fire, like the sun, provides us with light shining through each one of us and each plant on the earth. It illuminates our darkness, our earth and our humanity. The fire, like a candle, feeds us with tenderness of heart, provides us with the light of hope, and charges us with love and compassion for ourselves and others. The fire inside us gives us inspiration to create, provides fuel to ignite our dense body to reveal the light, and helps us to see through the layers of darkness, shadows, and *samskaras*. The fire itself is the light of consciousness and the light of awareness by which everything is known and everything is transformed and transmuted.

When the beauty of the earth is experienced by our sense organs, it fills our hearts with mirth. Mother earth nurtures us, mother earth takes away what we do not need, mother earth takes away the things that no longer serve us, mother earth lives inside each layer of our body, and mother earth is who we are. When we connect to the earth, we feel a sense of groundedness, a sense of belonging, and a sense of joy and love.

When the beauty of the rain touches our skin, it washes away all our pain. The water purifies us, the water cleanses us, the water neutralizes us, the water beholds us, and the water is who we are. As matter of fact, 75 percent of our body is made out of water. When we connect to the beauty of water, we experience the fluidity and flow of life, we reflect the beauty of the universe in everything and in everyone, we host all life forms, and we activate all creations and manifestations.

When the beauty of the vast sky becomes who we are, it teaches our minds to fly. The beauty of the sky has unlimited and boundless potential and possibilities. Only our conditioned minds limit our creative potentials. When we are bound with and become the sky, we float in the vast emptiness of the universe above all manifestations, we start seeing the world from the perspective of flying eyes, we sense the world and even ourselves as the vastness of the sky, we start creating the world and our lives like the beauty of the sky.

Ancient Wisdom

Siddha Master Gurumayi Chidvilasananda: Once the fountain of love is unlocked in our hearts, we see the magnificence of our existence. With that love we turn this world into a paradise.

Practice

1. Sing "Walk in Beauty" first thing in the morning when you wake up and also before you go to sleep.

2. Start seeing beauty, speaking beauty, thinking beauty, acting beauty, and walking beauty in a sacred way and in each and every day.

3. Create and accumulate a bundle of words of beauty in your vocabulary and write them down on your desk, bedside, daily planner, and grooves in your mind.

4. Merge or shape-shift yourself into fire, water, earth, air, and space; experience the characteristics of each element, and ask what lesson you learn from each of the elements.

Feed the Wolf
Create your own destiny

Story

Once upon a time, a grandfather told a story to his grandson: There were two wolves living inside his heart and constantly fighting; one is filled with envy, anger, hatred and fear; the other one is full of joy, love, compassion, grace, and light. "Who wins in your heart?" the grandson asked. "The one I feed."

Teaching

When we feed the anger we become the anger. When we feed envy we become envy. When we feed hatred we become hatred. When we feed fear we become fear. We human beings have similar downward spiral experiences in life when we are entangled in dramas and the darkness of our existence. We sometimes seem to not able to get out of the trap, the deep human suffering hole, because we do not actually realize that we feed the human suffering, the angry wolf, constantly and unconsciously.

When we feed the light we become the light. When we feed grace we become grace. When we feed love we become love. When we feed compassion we become compassionate. When we stay high in spirit we experience nothing but light.

We have the choice in life to feed the wolf of our liking. The wolf we feed shapes our inner landscape as who we are and who we are becoming. It also shapes the outer landscape that we are experiencing in this world as a reflection of our inner landscape and experiences. What we experience in the outer world is nothing but the creation and manifestation of our own inner paradigm.

The food we eat, thoughts we foster, actions we take, words we speak, friends we choose, paths we take, jobs we seek, partners we intuit to be destined with, emotions we choose to experience, and the life we create to live have an adverse effect on our inner and outer lives. So start feeding our heart with love, compassion, grace, joy, gratitude, oneness, harmony, and then we become the light of all qualities.

Ancient Wisdom

Sutra 1.33: The mind becomes pure and calm by cultivating friendliness toward the happy, compassion for the unhappy, delight toward the virtuous, and benevolent indifference toward the unrighteous.

Practice

1. List all positive and inspirational words in your notebook, day planner, desk, bedside, etc.
2. Fill your heart with nothing but love and light.
3. Speak kind and loving words to yourself and others.
4. Perform selfless acts for others and for humanity.
5. Choose and walk on the path of joy and love.
5. Sing the beauty, see the beauty, walk the beauty, speak the beauty, and be the beauty.
6. By the end of day, check which wolf you feed the most and experience how you feel?

Dismemberment
Mystical experience of oneness

Story

There was a story that came from the teaching of Tao that took place over 2000 years ago between Lao Tzu and his student, Yen. "I have made some progress," said Yen. "What do you mean?" asked Lao Tzu. "I have forgotten my ego and my culture," Replied Yen. "Very good, but it is not enough," said Lao Tzu. On another day Yen saw Lao Tzu again and said, "I have made some progress." "What do you mean?" asked Lao Tzu. "I have forgotten humanity and righteousness," replied Yen. "Very good, but not enough," Lao Tzu commented. Another day Yen met Lao Tzu again and said, "I have made some progress." "What do you mean?" inquired Lao Tzu. Yen responded, "I forget everything while sitting down." Lao Tzu's face turned pale and asked, "What do you mean by sitting down and forgetting everything?" "I cast aside my limbs," replied Yen, "discard my intellect, detach from both body and mind, become one with Tao – the Great Universe. This is what I called sitting down and forgetting everything." Lao Tzu said, "When you become one with the Great Universe, you have no partiality, and when you are part of the process of transformation, you will have no identity. You have become a wise man and I beg you continue on your soul journey."

Teaching

The practice and process of dismemberment is a cross-cultural, universal, and mystical phenomenon of clearing away and dissolving all the aspects of our humanness — of our earthly self, of our egoic make-up, of our *karma*, of our mind and body — that keeps us from remembering our connection to and experience with the divinity and the creative source from which we came. We all have such an experience consciously or unconsciously through meditation, dreamless deep sleep, zone sensation, and even near-death experience, even though we may not recognize the mystical encounters. It is, for most spiritual practices, the ultimate goal of the human race to reveal and experience the mystery of human revelation and soul evolution.

When we no longer identify ourselves with our bodies, our thoughts, our minds, our senses organs, our egos, our cultures, our beliefs, and our values, we merge ourselves into one with the mystical universe. In that experience we not only 'become one with' the universal consciousness but we *are* the universal consciousness. We as a human body experience the sense of bodiless, senseless, egoless, harmony, love, expansiveness, boundless, vastness, deathless, and emptiness yet fullness at the same time. We as a spiritual body experience the sense of union, oneness, light, *samadhi*, and liberation. I wonder who does not want to experience or at least have a glimpse of that mystery and 'unknown' in our western belief system.

What keeps us from experiencing the mystery is the belief system through which we have been cultured and "educated." We have been taught that there is nonexistence if we cannot see it. It is the foundation of today's "evidence-based science" approach. "Do not talk to your fairy friends, there is nothing there," we grew up and learned. Religious groups of the western world put intermediaries between the universal consciousness and the human race that keep us separated from oneness with all that exists. In order to experience oneness with the universal consciousness, we have to learn to embody the absolute and transmute, transform, and transcend our perception of separateness and our limiting belief system.

Ancient Wisdom

Atma Bodha, by Shankaracharya, Sutra 15: One should, through discrimination, separate the pure and inmost Self from the sheaths by which it is covered, as one separates a rice-kernel from the covering husk by striking it with a pestle.

Practice

1. Practice dismemberment meditation to experience mystical oneness by dissolving one body part at a time, from physical body, sense organs, emotions, thoughts, and the mind.

2. Take the Shamanic journey, if you are familiar with it, and ask your helping spirit to dismember your human self and take you to the place of manifestation.

3. Experience bodilessness and mindlessness when you are in deep sleep, in the zone, or in your daily meditation session.

4. Join and participate in a spiritual ceremony, like *satsang*, chanting, church singing, fire ceremony, or drum circle to experience the mystical oneness.

Harmony

The source of manifestations

Story

Once upon a time, there was a remote Chinese village that was suffering from extended drought. Every kind of prayer had been offered to put an end to the drought, but nothing had worked and the people were desperate. The only remaining option was to fetch a well-known rainmaker from a remote area in the mountain. When the wise old man arrived in a covered cart, he aligned himself with and sniffed the air in disdain and then asked for a cottage on the outskirts of the village. He insisted that he be totally undisturbed and that his food be left outside his door. Nobody heard from him for three days and then the village awoke to a downpour of rain mixed with snow, which was unheard of for that time of year.

The villagers were greatly impressed and approached to the wise old man, who was out of seclusion then. "So you can make rain, sir!" inquired the villagers. "No, I cannot make rain," the wise old man scoffed. "What do you mean? There was the most persistent drought until you came. Within three days it rained," objected the villagers. "Oh," responded the wise old man, "You see, I come from a region where everything is in order and harmony; it rains when it should and the people there are in order and harmony. But that was not the case when I arrived here. People here were out of order and harmony, or "Tao," and I was immediately infected so I had to be quiet and alone until I was once more in harmony with Tao and then, naturally, it rained."

Teaching

When we are not in harmony within ourselves and when we are not in alignment with the elements of the world around us, we experience separation and a split from the fullness of life – rain does not fall, scarcity and lacking are experienced in life, stress and anxiety are expressed every day, and even illnesses are manifested as a result. When we are in harmony within and without, we experience the walk-in-beauty, we experience the oneness, we experience fullness, we experience the abundance, we experience ecstasy, and we even experience wonders and miracles in life.

Harmony is when we are aligned with everything in order. Harmony is expressed in all aspects of life within ourselves – we eat what our body needs, not what we crave; we drink the pure nectar of fruits and the earth, not the toxins; we speak the sweetness from the loving and compassionate heart, not to hurt someone; we think of the Divine and our purpose for living here, to experience our soul evolution; and we act selflessly to serve humanity, not to feed the egoic self. Harmony is also expressed outside us – we respect and work with the mother earth, not control and manipulate her; we follow the flow of the river and the season changes and earthly evolution, not against and not to alter.

Life itself, the planet earth herself, and even individuals themselves are always in harmony, in full, and in perfection. Just like the moon, it is always full, even when it appears not to be. Just like the sun, it always shines, even we experience darkness. Just like hummingbird, she always drinks the nectar of flowers, even in the dark gray winter. And just like the life we live, there is always abundance and happiness, even when we experience scarcity and illness. The state of union, harmony, perfection, fullness, abundance, love and compassion is the birthright of our existence. Everything manifested in our lives is expressed in many forms that may appear different from the intention and the source of the creation due to the dressed up layers and shadows that we experience through the ego, conditioned mind, and cultural beliefs and values. It is up to us to shed and see through the layers and illusions, to sense, to experience, and to be in union and oneness with all that is manifested, and even un-manifested, of the divinity. This is the ultimate purpose of the human race.

Modern Harmony

Many of us have been to a symphony concert. We notice the first thing that happens is the concertmaster (first violinist) appears, and plays one note on the violin. That note is A below Middle C that resonates at the frequency of 440 cycles per second. This is the note that all the concert players will attune to for the duration of the performance. Not getting in on this attunement to the fundamental frequency will cause the errant musician to be out of tune with the music even if he plays the correct notes from the music score. The rare musician who has perfect pitch just *knows* where A-440 is.

A-440 is the source frequency that is at the root of the fundamental harmonies for all music in the west. In the same way, the stillness of meditation shines the source energy of consciousness that permeates all perception in all life everywhere. It is the source of universal wisdom that projects itself in every thought and every action that we do. We will be in perfect harmony with all other players who are thus attuned to this source energy.

Those who do not resonate with this source energy will be in perpetual dissonance, reflected by the thoughts and actions of the player, even though they might have the same music in front of them as other players in the drama.

It is so fundamental to our life and 'being' to be rooted in the source state of consciousness. All it takes is just a few minutes every day in meditation to re-tune to the concertmaster and get on the right frequency for the performance of the day. Through practice, we will 'just know' where the space of attunement is, and live from that place always.

Practice

1. Sing a harmonious song in your heart all the time. It could come from your intuition or could be learned. Here is a sample song: "Earth my body, water my blood, air my breath, fire my spirit."

2. Create and be in union and harmony within yourself in terms of the food you eat, words you speak, thoughts you think, work you do, and actions you take in your everyday life. Ask yourself, "Am I in harmony within myself?"

3. Create and be in union and harmony with the world around you, the people, the earth, the wind, the water, the fire, the space, the season, and the planet in your everyday life. Ask yourself, "Am I in harmony with the world around me?"

4. Create and be in union and oneness with the love 'n' light of divinity. Ask yourself, "Do I feel separated and split from the love 'n' light?"

5. Create a simple ritual for yourself in every morning and night to remember the unity and harmony of the life you live inside and outside.

References and Recommended Readings

Armstrong, Karen. *The Spiral Staircase: My Climb Out of Darkness.* Anchor Books, 2004.

Birch, Beryl. *Power Yoga.* Fireside Books, 1995.

Chopra, Deepak. *Ageless Body, Timeless Mind.* Three Rivers Press, 1994.

Cumes, Carol and Romulo Lizarraga Valencia. *Journey to Machu Picchu: Spiritual Wisdom from the Andes.* Magical Journey Publishing, 2005.

Delgado, Jorge Luis. *Andean Awakening: An Inca Guide to Mystical Peru.* Council Oak Books, 2006.

Devananda. Vishnu. *Meditation and Mantra.* Motilal Banarsidass, 2000.

Devananda. Vishnu. *The Complete Illustrated Book of Yoga.* Three Rivers Press, 1988.

Diaz, Edwin Rogelio Cuevas. Imprenta "ALVAREZ", La Resistencia De La Cultura En La Colonia A Traves De La Simbologia Andina, Av. Jorge Carrasco North 68. 2000.

Douillard, John. *Body, Mind and Sport: The Mind-Body Guide to Lifelong Fitness and Your Personal Best.* Harmony, 1994.

Emoto, Masaru. *The Secret Life of Water.* Atria Books, 2005.

Fields, Rick, Peggy Taylor, Rex Weyler, and Rick Ingrasci. *Chop Wood, Carry Water*. Tarcher, 1984.

Frawley, David. *Ayruvedic Healing*. Lotus Press, 2001.

Frawley, David. *Vedantic Meditation*. North Atlantic, 2000.

Hanh, Thich Nhat. *Collection: One Spirit*, Bantam Books ad Parallax Press, 1991.

Hanh, Thich Nhat. *Present Moment Wonderful Moment: Mindfulness Verses for Daily Living*. Full Circle, 1990.

Hill, Dennis. *The Inner Yoga of Happiness*. Trafford Publishing, 2008.

Hill, Dennis. *Yoga Sutras: The Means to Liberation*. Trafford Publishing, 2007.

Iyengar, B. K. S. *Light on Yoga*. Schocken Books, 1995.

Krishnamurti, Jiddu. *The First and Last Freedom*. Harper, 1954.

Krishnamurti, Jiddu. *Total Freedom*. Harper, 1996.

Melchizedek, Drunvalo. *Serpent of Light: Beyond 2012: The Movement of the Earth's Kundalini and the Rise of the Female Light 1949 to 2013*. Weiser Books, 2007.

Prabhavananda, Swami, and Christopher Isherwood. *Shankara's Crest-Jewel of Discrimination (Viveka-Chudamani)*. Vedanta Press, 1978.

Redfield, James. *The Celestine Prophecy*. Warner Books, 1993.

Redfield, James. *The Secret of Shambhala: In Search of the Eleventh Insight*, Warner Books, 1999.

Roberts, Llyn, and Robert Levy. *Shamanic Reiki: Expanded Ways of Working with Universal Life Force Energy*. O Books, 2008.

Rumi. *The Essential Rumi*. Trans. Coleman Barks. Harper, 1995.

Schiffmann, Erich. *Yoga: The Spirit and Practice of Moving into Stillness.* Pocket Books, 1996.

Sivananda, Swami. *Conquest of Mind.* Divine Life Society, 2002.

Sivananda, Swami. *Practice of Vedanta.* Divine Life Society, 2000.

Sivananda, Swami. *The Principal Upanishads.* Divine Life Society, 1998.

Sivananda, Swami. *Thought Power.* Divine Life Society, 2004.

Sivananda, Swami. *Vedanta: (Jnana Yoga).* Divine Life Society, 1987.

The Sivananda Yoga Center. *The Sivananda Companion to Meditation.* Simon & Schuster, 2000.

The Sivananda Yoga Center. *The Sivananda Companion to Yoga.* Simon & Schuster, 2000.

Tolle, Eckhart. *The Power of Now: A Guide to Spiritual Enlightenment.* New World Library, 1990.

Villoldo, Alberto. *Courageous Dreaming: How Shamans Dream the World into Being.* Hay House, 2008.

Villoldo, Alberto. *Mending the Past and Healing the Future with Soul Retrieval.* Hay House, 2005.

Villoldo, Alberto. *The Four Insights: Wisdom, Power, and Grace of the Earthkeepers.* Hay House, 2005.

Villoldo, Alberto and Erik Jendresen. *Dance of the Four Winds: Secrets of the Inca Medicine Wheel.* Destiny Books, 1995.

Villoldo, Alberto and Erik Jendresen. *Island of the Sun: Mastering the Inca Medicine Wheel.* Destiny Books, 1995.

Yogananda, Paramahansa. *Autobiography of a Yogi.* Crystal Clarity, 1946.